Edward H Kaeele

Friends,
Partners,
and Lovers

S0-CAA-137

Friends, Partners, and Lovers

A Good Word About Marriage

Warren Lane Molton

Judson Press® Valley Forge

FRIENDS, PARTNERS, AND LOVERS

Copyright © 1979
Judson Press, Valley Forge, PA 19481

All rights reserved. No part of this publication may be reproduced, stored in a retrieval system, or transmitted in any form or by any means, electronic, mechanical, photocopying, recording, or otherwise, without the prior permission of the copyright owner, except for brief quotations included in a review of the book.

Library of Congress Cataloging in Publication Data

Molton, Warren Lane.
  Friends, partners, and lovers.

  Bibliography: p. 153
  1. Marriage.   2. Interpersonal relations.   3. Self-
actualization (Psychology)   I. Title.
HQ734.M79   301.42   78-24435
ISBN 0-8170-0815-2

The name JUDSON PRESS is registered as a trademark in the U.S. Patent Office.
Printed in the U.S.A. ⊕

S. WARD

For Dian

Friend, Partner, and Lover

FOREWORD

Books," someone has said, "are men's hearts in other men's hands." This is a beautiful thought, but not always true. Books are often written to make money, to get attention, to demonstrate scholarship. Many writers would be quite reluctant to commit their hearts to the hands of their readers.

Some books, however, *are* written out of loving concern for the well-being of others. And this, I believe, is one of them. I therefore appreciate the invitation to explore it in advance of its other readers, and the opportunity to commend it to them.

In my lifetime I have read a great many books for a good many reasons. A goodly proportion of those books have been about marriage, because that has been my field of specialized study. Some books have been long, heavy, and academic. Others have been short, light, and superficial. Between these extremes, books on marriage exist in as great variety as do books on every other subject.

This one, I believe, has special merit. Let me tell you why I think so.

Unquestionably, Warren Molton knows his subject. He is a qualified and experienced marital therapist. In these pages we meet many of the husbands and wives who have sought his help; and we catch illuminating glimpses of how he tried to help them. Obviously he is a sensitive, perceptive, and caring person, who meets human need with sympathetic understanding, with insight, and with quiet confidence that there are resources available to people who are in trouble.

Further, he speaks about marriage against a background of successful and deeply rewarding personal experience. He dedicates the book to his wife, Dian; and she, in a moving preface, adds her testimony to his, that as a couple they have built a healthy and happy marriage of their own. Not all who write about marriage have personally succeeded in it, or even experienced it; but for me, there is a special authenticity about an author who offers knowledge to others that has been applied successfully to his own life situation.

Another merit of the book is that its author knows how to write. If need be, I am ready to learn from a person whose communication skills are not by any means what I could wish for. However, it is a special pleasure to sit at the feet of a man who has acquired dexterity in the use of the English language. Warren Molton certainly has done that. Again and again, I paused to savor an apt phrase or a pleasing passage. Here are a few that arrested my attention. He speaks of "cherishables that become perishables"; of a "raw, chin-into-the wind courage that is sheer foolishness." He says that "the tongue is an army of little samplers," and that "a total woman is a partial person." He describes history as "strewn with corpses of those who died in our grisly battles over definitions of the good life." Such felicitous phrasing makes for a book that is a sheer pleasure to read.

Finally, the book is put together with real artistry. It reminded me, somehow, of a favorite piece of music—Mussorgsky's *Pictures at an Exhibition*. Without ever losing his clear sense of direction, the author takes us on a meandering tour, stopping from time to time to point out something special or to explain something difficult. He illuminates familiar words like intimacy, caring, cherishing, celebration, communication, and transcendence, giving them new significance. He sketches a diagram to make his meaning clear and makes a point by throwing in true-to-life snatches of husband-wife conversations. He reports fantasies from couples who took part in his programs and even throws in a quiz to help us to examine how we rate feminine and masculine characteristics. He scatters pearls of wisdom from a richly stored mind, unostentatiously commenting on matters of philosophy or theology or literature; and he mingles his prose with flights of poetic imagery.

All this adds up to a delightfully readable book. I commend it to students of marriage as a thought-provoking source of sound material; to the general reader who in these days hears a bewildering babel of conflicting voices and really wants to know where marriage is; but most of all, I commend it to husbands and wives, as a beautiful gift they could offer to each other, reading it together, talking over what they learn, and using it as a stimulus for ongoing growth in their relationship.

David R. Mace

CONTENTS

PREFACE

When Warren asked me to read this manuscript with the thought in mind of writing a Preface, I was pleased because it gave me an opportunity to think through and write down what I thought about both the book and marriage. Since I often experience the "other side" of his counseling, the constant sorting of what is valid, what might work, what is overromanticized, what causes pain and failure, perhaps my reflections might have their place.

Warren and I seem to have survived the stress of the hardest years when children were young, money was scarce, professional ambitions shifting, and attitudes about roles under close scrutiny. So hurray for us! A good many talented, sensitive, bright, and able people didn't make it. Does that make us sound smug or self-congratulatory to people in real pain who struggle daily just to hold on? God forbid! Some of our personal marriage history, I am sure, was just dumb luck. Out of two vastly different cultural backgrounds, with conflicting ambitions and strong egos, we chose each other and made a covenant with our inflated optimism and gut-level chemistry. Other people with similar packages of emotional dynamite blew it after a few years. Some lived happy, productive lives unmarried. Some tried again, and put two or even three sets of children together to form other marriages, and failed again. Is the institution, with all its enormous risks and burdens, still a constructive way to do life? Our children talk about "alternative life-styles," and they offer some creative methods of getting needs met. Yet for me, and for many other adults, marriage is possible within a context of freedom, maturity, and nurturance. I know it is possible to be self-sufficient and still enjoy the delicate, mystical balance of daily life shared with another person in community and intimacy.

To be married at age twenty meant, for me, to invest my hopes for happiness and my fears of failure in another person, and to expect all good things to come forth—a heavy burden for the partner! Most young people know better now. They are more cautious—and they should be. Most of them seem to know themselves better than we did, and perhaps if and when they establish permanent relationships, they might be spared some of the pain of figuring all of that out in concert with a partner. Yet in the caution that steers clear of commitment, I see some very lonely people who might have been able to learn to grow in the context of love and caring, with some honest warmth and human intimacy. These still seem to be the elements we need and deserve as human beings, and which we are capable of giving and receiving if we can just learn how to do it.

I remember two women sitting on a porch one hot afternoon. One of them was my mother. Her visitor said, "Well, I've had four husbands. Buried two and dumped two."

"That's hard," said my mother, and then she added by way of contrast, "I've been married to the same man for thirty years."

"That's hard, too," said her friend.

"Yes," said my mother.

I don't think anyone finds marriage absolutely smooth sailing for thirty years, or twenty, or one. Most adults have about all they can handle, one way or another. For me, doing marriage with Warren is the energy-giving core of my life, from which my professional and intellectual energies spin off. It is the center. But it didn't just "happen" that way. Doris Lessing once wrote that women may find it impossible to put up with the discrimination, chauvinism, and insults they encounter every day and process them without bitterness unless there is a stable, life-giving relationship going on with a man that gives balance to the rest of it. For me, this is true and is one of the reasons that finding out what is good about marriage, what it can do for us, and how we can find ways to enjoy it have been so worthwhile for both of us.

My single friends report to me that what they like *best* about being single is the freedom to come and go as they choose. Yet, most of them have children, and so they are not totally free to do that anyway. What they seem to like *least* is the fear of being totally alone when they are older. They also worry about inflicting the demands of their loneliness on their children. Yet that happens in marriage as well as among single parents. The questions and conflicts on both sides of the matrimonial road seem to be constantly shifting from one side to the other.

I think that one thing which might help women would be hearing from successful professional women who like being married and seem to manage homes, children, and marriages competently. There are those who genuinely feel that marriage helps them grow and enhances their lives. I hope the women's movement will help us explore this with maturity and astute observation. To look into the literature on marriage these days is often an experience that offers somebody else's pompous "here's how," either a solution so patronizingly self-righteous that it is embarrassing, or one which is a humiliating put-down for either men or women.

I believe there is an adult society being fashioned that can handle marriage, parenting, personal freedom, growth, and genuine usefulness to society. I believe we are fashioning this kind of adult out of the various new therapies, the women's movement, the new-age communities, and the experimental educationists, who explore and design new ways of living and learning that are both human and effective.

What Warren and his colleagues are trying to do is not to "patch up" a decadent system that happens to be called "marriage." It is an effort to help people do a more creative thing—a way of making life good between marriage partners in today's society. They are trying to find the tools to do this and accurately to name these tools.

What they are doing, and what Warren and I have been struggling to refine, name, and check for *reality* and *workableness* has very little to do with "marriage" as my parents did it, or his parents, or many of our friends. It is not a game for children, a temporary oasis for the single-minded, nor a formula for filling up the emptiness of boredom, loneliness, or emotional bankruptcy.

I read *Friends, Partners, and Lovers* all the way through today. I believe it is a book of realistic hope. That it happens to be the model that worked for us is incidental, because it came not just from our efforts, but from the whole spectrum of human struggle and celebration that crosses the threshold of Warren's office every day. From them we also learn. People still want to be married; they want marriages that are permanent, and marriages that nurture and fulfill rather than destroy their personhood. It is worth the effort.

Dian Molton

INTRODUCTION

Marriage is being challenged on every side. It is rejected as inhibiting, obsolete, useless, and ridiculous. Some say that marriage is whatever a couple agree it is. For these reasons, I have with humor called marriage an alternative life-style. Yet most of the voices calling for change are instructive and deserve our attention.

This book is yet another voice. Its message is simple. While marriage is in trouble, our biggest problem is not the institution but the instruction. We are not taught how to do marriage, and most of our models are faulty. This book is not intended as a catechism for all couples but, rather, one simple model that may be useful for those trying to make marriage a creative venture.

When I speak here of marriage, I speak of men and women promising to do life together for life. Permanence is not guaranteed. People and circumstances change, often radically. Hence, there must always be appropriate ways to set aside promises with dignity. Still, the intention is the old one: permanence. While I shall outline some of the how and why, I want even more for us to understand the *who* of marriage, the men and women who are attempting to get real life-needs met over the span of a lifetime with one another, in the three enormously complex and exciting worlds of friend, partner, and lover.

Marriage is the most exciting relationship of my life. It calls for more of me than anything else, and the woman of that marriage maintains the dialogue with great energy and creativity, so that to do marriage with her is deeply fulfilling. Beyond that, Dian is so much a part of all the rest of me—work, children, friends, and the whole search for meaning. And she plays so well! If there were no such thing as marriage, I would be doing something just like it with her anyway.

Here I as author and we as mates want to share something of what we have discovered together. Still, life expands. We lay no claims to having arrived. We are simply well embarked upon a good sea. Where it leads we are not certain. We enjoy our fantasy of the future. But life is fickle, and we see ahead so poorly. The *covenant* we keep is to do life together always. The *contract* changes. Today it says, "Let's do the contract *this* way." Yet, tomorrow we may change the contract to fit tomorrow's emerging needs, in order that we might continue to say, "Life together is good."

It is our hope that this sketch of two people married and marrying anew each day will be helpful to others. Our expectations of this relationship will not be right or good for every couple. It is a little like reporting a vacation trip to friends who went there themselves. We visited many of the same places, all of the special ones, but our experiences were quite different. They *should* be. That is all the more reason for sharing. We welcome hearing about *your* trip.

I want to express my deepest gratitude to family and friends who have graciously shared in so many ways in the preparation of this book: the dedication is to Dian because without her the book would not be; then our children, Stephen, Jennifer, and David, who give much purpose and joy to our marriage and understand us amazingly well; my parents, Hiram and Wilhelmina, for their beautiful marriage and love; Dian's parents, George and Ruth Elledge, for creating her; Bob Mann, Carole Raines, and Sheelagh Bull who read and fed back as I wrote, offering many good ideas; Bob Carrigan for suggestions regarding transcendence; colleagues, Tom Green, Ramon Corrales, and Arthur Foster, for their support and encouragement; friends and typists, Karen Ahearne, Susan Oster, Debbie Yeo, and Connie Highley; and finally, a word of appreciation to my clients and students over the years who deeply disclosed the joy and pain of their own marriages. All of you share whatever good may be offered in the pages of this book.

Warren Lane Molton
Kansas City, Missouri

AUTONOMY: KEY TO *1* THE ADULT PERSON

The most crucial element in the creation of a healthy marriage is the healthy adult, and the truly healthy adult is autonomous. To be autonomous is to be in charge of my own life. I belong to me. I accept responsibility for me. I command my life and sit in the driver's seat. I am not on my knees in the back looking out the window at what someone else has driven me through. Nor am I even in the passenger's seat up front sharing the decisions and viewing firsthand where I am going. I am, rather, behind the wheel, keeping my life on the road, and moving toward my destination. If I do not belong to me, I belong to someone else.

I may, of course, commit myself to another person, some great cause, a personal task, or a religion. Still, I must begin by owning me. Since I cannot give that which I do not own, I must first establish ownership of myself, taking charge of me, and commanding my life. Then I may freely give myself to a relationship transcending me.

Some of us may still belong to our parents, even though we call ourselves adults. They own us, setting out goals, making decisions, and offering unsolicited criticism. They may use their own hurt feelings, anger, money, ill humor, ridicule, or rejection in order to maintain control over us. They may even rule us from the grave.

Knuckling under to what Eric Berne has called Criticial Parent tapes may keep us childish and enslaved and can prevent us from becoming autonomous adults.

Even religion can direct our lives without becoming an integral part of our own belief system. It can be a mechanical process by which we simply obey religious laws, rituals, and expectations in the community. We may uncritically carry out religious orders like obedient children; or we may agree that certain religious behavior is required, and so we ritually obey. Religion ought to have personal meaning, a meaning which I understand and cherish. It is not enough that it is meaningful for my parents, or that my mate needs and wants it, or that I should be a good example to my children. Religion is my personal attempt to understand the meaning of my life. The idea of religion as the "friendly cop" is repulsive. Nor is religion the "handbook" or "multiplication table" by which I transact my purchase of life. It is not my governor, keeper, or jailer. Rather, my religion is like a friend, whom I love, and with whom I attempt to understand and do life. I can embrace this friend. I may also challenge and debate my friend. We may even have to part company, briefly or forever. My friend does not own me.

Some of us *belong* to a vocational group, a business organization, a club or neighborhood. The control of goals and patterns is relinquished to the *other,* so that we are held captive by that group and dare not make a move at odds with the group. A man once told me: "We have a block party every Labor Day, and, boy, you just decide to do something other than go to that party, and I'll swear they'd egg your house. Your own *neighbors!* Your *friends!"*

We can be under the rule of spouse or children. We defer to them and feel manipulated. Any sense of "I belong to me" is lost. There is no time for privacy. A woman locks herself in her bathroom every morning for half an hour to "escape my two- and three-year-olds." A man angrily said to me, "We didn't have our children. They had us. To take care of them. To give, give, give. Well, I've had it. I've been *had* enough." If our spouse or children own us, it is our fault. We let it happen. We may even have asked for it, until it got out of hand. There are many ways to be owned, all of which deny autonomy.

The situation may develop quite innocently. In one instance, a divorced woman married a second time and her new husband moved in with her. The mortgage was held by her father, who had helped her keep the house for the sake of her twin sons. Eventually the new husband resented the house, her father, and his wife. His feelings of being an equal partner were destroyed. Father had a say in everything regarding the property, refusing to sell the house to the couple for fear that the new husband might also leave his daughter and get an unfair share of the property, including father's investment. The husband was not autonomous in that arrangement. He felt owned by his father-in-law, and the very thing this parent most feared was coming to pass because of his paranoia about daughter's husband. The young husband's feeling of being trapped and controlled brought them into counseling. His sense of helplessness soon turned to rage at the father-in-law, leading to a major confrontation with him, and a settlement which restored ownership to the couple. The marriage suffered great stress during this process.

A *negative* check for autonomy is the "Who is to blame?" question. The blaming person does not feel in charge. Problems are not solved but are transferred to someone else or to circumstances. If we, in the face of setback, accuse someone for the situation we have not yet taken in hand, we are looking for a scapegoat. The blaming person needs an excuse, an out, for not assuming responsibility.

A *positive* check for autonomy has to do with taking an inventory of our own resources. How do I handle being alone? Can I meet normal financial obligations? Do I get problems solved? Am I an action person? Do I take care of my body? Am I aware of my emotional needs and how to get them met without exploiting someone else, or getting "ripped off"? Do I live creatively in my environment without exhausting myself or the gifts of that environment? Or do I say, "If only I had been born rich, or beautiful, or talented, or into a great family"? Being in charge of my own life means to know and understand the universe of me and how I can best command my destiny with the resources available to me. I do not complain about what has been done to me. Life is not an "If only . . ." but a "What if. . . ?" Risk is the key.

Adults are those who have achieved significant autonomy, are their own caretakers, and believe that success or failure is mostly in their own hands. There is always the possibility of personal disaster resulting from circumstances beyond our control, but the goal is to remain in charge of self. It is hard to imagine a price too high to pay in order to maintain *autonomy: personal freedom with responsibility among one's peers.*

One of the tragedies of our culture is that most of our systems foster dependency. Any time we create cookie-cutter-look-alikes, we reduce personal and individual initiative, energy, and imagination. We then teach people to function as labor parts of a gigantic machine, or sheep in theological systems, or apprentices to stereotyped professions, or voters in dehumanizing political power blocks. We destroy the individual's right to discover his or her own life. It is not strange, then, that at the sophisticated peak of computerized civilization in the twentieth century, some of our brightest and most creative young people have returned to the soil, using simple methods and tools to create a life-supporting farm, giving enormous time and energy to the simple tasks of growing and harvesting, nurturing and protecting. And when asked why, we hear, "To belong to me, to be my own person, and to experience the basic survival of *me*."

It is not necessarily true that these young people have an answer to our ills, but they are at least posing alternatives to the dependency syndrome. Among the most cherished and established professions of medicine, law, education, and ministry, the quest for autonomy has created mavericks who open free clinics, are legal counselors for the poor and disfranchised, start schools without walls and churches in homes. They are responding to a need to feel empowered and to give individuals the feeling of being in charge of their personal destiny. An old woman, who might have lived longer than she did, refused to go to a hospital because "They take over more than's theirs."

Autonomy may suggest to some that marriage is obsolete. They might assume that the autonomous person cannot enter into any relationship that diminishes personal autonomy. To say this is to miss the point. Autonomy does not foreclose relational contracts. Rather, the individual is better equipped to enter the relationship freely and creatively. He or she now can be an adult, with a power field to commit to other strong, autonomous persons. Together they effect an alliance of strength and resources that can facilitate private and corporate goals. They invite, encourage, and enable one another. Their common good is bound up in the realization of each other's potential. They are free to negotiate from self-knowledge and are then able to relinquish and exchange gifts without reserve or defensiveness.

Perspective: Inner-Directed

The perspective, or life-view, of the autonomous adult is that of the *inner-directed* person, suggested by David Riesman in *The Lonely Crowd,* and is contrasted with the *outer-* and *other-* directed person.

The *inner-directed* adult views life from *this side of things.* The outlook is from inside *out,* one which says, "I view life from my own door, and I seek my way in terms of my own basic needs, with an enlightened concern for others. To face life realistically, I must be able to view it out of my history, and from my spot in the world." It was with these feelings that a young man declined his father's offered gift of the "lot next door," on which to build his home, and said, "My father's world and mine are very different, and walking out on the same street to pick up the same paper every morning won't change the outlook."

If I am *outer-directed,* I determine my way according to what others want of me. By seeking out their desires, I am distracted from me and may very well lose touch with myself, ignore my talents, and miss my own destiny. A premedical student was the third child of a family in which her mother and father and older brothers were all physicians. She was also engaged to a medical student. While in college she had enjoyed acting and wanted to pursue a master's degree in theater. Her fiancé was sympathetic but disappointed, and her own family ridiculed the idea with open laughter. Her parents finally said that they would not finance such a program. After college graduation, she fell into depression, broke her engagement, and took a nonlethal overdose of drugs. Her pretense at suicide was a protest against the helpless feeling of being controlled by the expectations of others. Clearly, she was not ready for marriage.

After a little more than three months of therapy, she liked herself better, told her parents she was never going into medicine, concluded her relationship with her boyfriend, found a job, an apartment, and enrolled in the theater department of the local state university. She laughed one day and said, "Even my voice is stronger." Everything about her, even the way she walked, communicated strength and commitment. It is too soon yet to see where she goes with her dream, but she is a surer and happier person—in Maslow's language, a more "self-actualizing person." Her perspective moved from outside to inside.

The *other-directed* person is ruled by concepts of transcendence, such as "the will of God," or the Holy Other. The *other* may also be some special cause by which one's will is captured and ruled.

I have counseled seminary students who believed they were called into ministry at a very early age—perhaps as young as five years. They felt the decision was closed and should never be challenged. Occasionally, such single-minded commitment ignores serious deficits and may in fact even be confirmed as God's will *by* those very deficits, as did one student who stuttered. He said to me, "Moses probably stuttered. If God would call a stutterer, he must surely want him badly, and have something special for him to do. How can I not obey?" This man did nothing about correcting the stutter, refusing to enter therapy after his wife had brought him to a counselor one time. He was really not free to examine his life from any point if it challenged "God's call." It was a major defense system for him, and he was not going to venture out long enough to find out what freedom is about. At age eleven he had been "called" to the ministry. It was an obsession which preempted discussion of most of the critical life decisions and made him unavailable for serious debate regarding his wife's needs, where the children would be reared, salary problems, and other such subjects that threatened an absolute allegiance to the simple notion of "God's got me, and nothing else matters." How much better if he had been able to own himself and create relationships with a gift of himself. Instead, an overriding, absolute, blind obedience to one experience at age eleven determined *all* his relationships and left him in what he called his "happy prison." If his rage ever emerges, it will be an ugly thing to see. Now he has it contained in his "God box."

This man might be dismissed as a religious fanatic and not at all typical of commitment to some transcending person or cause. However, hardly a month passes that I do not see or hear of someone who has a similar obsession in other professions. Medicine occasionally has its own special sort of physician or nurse given to such messianic visions of self. Every cause has its saviors.

Again, the perspective of the autonomous adult is that of one who is inner-directed. To be such a person, or to be in the process of becoming such a person, means that I must be working at creating a person of unity and coherence. The elements of my ego bind together in an integrated whole, and I function inside and outside as one who is in fact, as we say, together.

Unity

Autonomy greatly depends upon my understanding of myself as a thinking, feeling, acting, and believing person. A helpful construct looks like this:

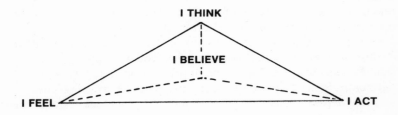

I understand *me* as I understand how I function in each of these areas. It may seem that my thinking and feeling decide my action. This is not always true, however, as it may be only when I *act* that I begin to know my real feelings or thinking. Recently I asked a man how his wife's anger made him feel. At the other end of the short sofa he said he did not know. With that she flung her arm out and bopped him on his shoulder. Needless to say, his feelings were quickly triggered. *Her* action tripped *his* feelings. This process is clear.

It is sometimes harder if our feelings are more deeply buried. It may be only by *acting* that these feelings thaw out and begin to emerge. It is like not knowing how you feel about cauliflower until you taste it. Often, to shake hands or touch someone's arm clarifies feelings. To begin talking may bring tears or relaxing laughter. Certain actions stimulate feelings and are like priming the feeling pump. It still amazes me when a couple, with frosty feelings and only polite communication, are willing to hold hands and gaze quietly at one another for a few moments, and are able then to find a flood of feelings. The touch of hand and eye opens the way.

Therefore, the triangle works in any direction, and it may start from any one of the three corners. Problems most often emerge when one corner of the triangle is in conflict with the other two. For example: Cover the *think* corner with your thumb. You are now working off the *feel-act* side (if it feels good, do it). This sounds like fun; but if the thinking process is blocked, you may be in trouble. A man was enjoying an affair until he suddenly thought, *This is exactly what my father was doing before Mother was killed in the auto wreck.* The *feeling-action* system was thrown into great *anxiety.* He became impotent, could not sleep, and lost considerable weight. His question was, "Why did it take two months for my head to plug into that situation?" A memory of his father triggered his own thought processes, which helped him reflect upon his *feeling-action* trap.

The relevance of the triangle can be further seen by covering either of the other two corners. If you cover *feel,* you work off the *think-act* side. Persons who block emotion in this way are often wooden and automatic. You never know their feelings. They keep feelings covered and may have a rather "blah" personality. If we block feelings, we may get into a rut. We become *routinized.* Life gets dull. We are trapped in a ritual. Recently an unhappy wife said, "I simply thought, 'you *are* married, now *act* married.' I did that for six years, and I have lost all my feelings for my husband. I buried them and one day I realized that they were gone." And with a bitter smile she concluded, "I guess my feelings just rotted." The result of blocking feelings is *apathy,* a "who cares?" attitude of indifference. To know and accept feelings is to open up the triangle and permit new action based on feeling demands. Her divorce might have come earlier, her marriage killed, rather than being allowed to rot. However, her marriage might also have been saved if she had honored her feelings and addressed her spouse with them.

Now cover the *action* corner. You say to your spouse, "I have a great idea that I am really excited about." You describe it and are then informed that your mate has no intention of doing such a thing, no matter how you feel about it. *Action* is blocked and the result is apt to be frustration and *anger.* The triangle wants to flow. We begin to hurt when one corner is blocked. If two are blocked or diminished, it registers in the personality, with varying consequences, usually with enormous stress that leaves the person immobilized. Healthy action is the most convincing message to the ego. Wants and needs are the *goals* of the triangle. "I want to make love because my *thinking* and *feeling* tell me that this is a pleasurable *act* that is congruent with my *beliefs* about the relationship."

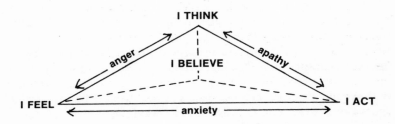

Still, the *I believe* at the center is the key to the healthy functioning of the adult person. This has to do with my values, priorities, commitments, and my own personal life vision, what Carl Jung called "one's own private myth." These make up the great integrating force of my life, bind me together as it were, and directly influence what I think, feel, and do. It is at this Center that I discover and declare the *meaning* of my life and perhaps in a philosophical or theological system set out my understanding of the meaning of my life. It is out of this Center that my thinking, feeling, and acting are molded. The Center directs, instructs, and equips the business of the other three areas. The Center carries the characteristics of an informing wisdom. It is not just a cop or jailer. The Center is more the honored maestro conducting the symphonic movements of the personality as a harmony of thought, feeling, and action mobilize the person to get life done with creativity and satisfaction. In marriage we are constantly seeking stimulation and compatibility in all of these areas. There must be enough congruence between husband and wife regarding life meaning, thinking process, feeling systems, and action to permit a fulfilling exchange.

A young couple, briefly married, found that the husband's new infatuation with bow-and-arrow hunting was creating problems. The wife saw it as a cruel sport that was quite unacceptable within her set of values. She resented everything about the sport, felt weepy on the days he hunted and angry when he came home, whether or not he had game. Quarrels resulted from this situation. It appeared to be an isolated problem, that is, not symptomatic of deeper problems. The wife discounted any other inquiry about her jealousy, stubbornness, and insinuations that seemed to attach to her concern over hunting. She retorted with statements, such as "Even a gun would not be quite so bad." She insisted that all killing is evil, but the arrow, as a "primitive and inaccurate" weapon, was torturous and obscene. It became clear that the marriage would not abide bow-and-arrow hunting. For the wife it was a value-ridden behavior, and, in order to preserve the tranquillity of the marriage, the husband finally decided to discontinue the sport. The relationship was immediately stabilized. He was disappointed but not spiteful, and his wife was obviously relieved and grateful. She had no fear of his being vindictive, and he exhibited no sign of feeling henpecked.

We all can cite similar examples of marital disharmony over drugs, alcohol, infidelity, gambling, or other behavior which may be unacceptable to a spouse. Many values are steadfast and are definitive aspects of persons. Clashes over values between mates may forecast disaster. Not all values can be checked out before marriage; they may come after marriage and should be newly contracted.

The belief system at the Center monitors, conditions, and, inversely, is also influenced by the other three systems—thinking, feeling, acting. Logic said to a young husband, whose wife was completely paralyzed after a skiing accident, that he should accept her suggestion that they divorce. However, the commitment at the Center, in dialogue with his reasoning processes, overrode his logic. He insisted that he loved her and would continue to be her husband. Such a decision affected the feelings that moved between them, and prescribed much of the action of the relationship. It conditioned plans for children, friendships, and their sex life. In fact, the entire relationship was profoundly changed by his decision to accept the impact of the accident and remain in the marriage. Another set of values, just as valid, might have caused a husband to accept his wife's offer, resulting in divorce, and a chance to create a new marriage.

A belief system may not confront the thinking or even the feeling systems, permitting them to function freely, yet totally block an action which would seem to be the obvious outcome of certain thought and feeling. For example, an attractive young woman had erotic fantasies about a man in her office. She honestly said, "I love him, am sexually aroused by him, and he is my male ideal. But he is happily married, so far as I can tell, and I will not take or allow action which might threaten that marriage. It is a matter of values. To consider an affair is selfish, destructive thinking which I reject, else I have trouble knowing who I am at the Center, where I locate conscience and personal dignity."

In terms of our triangle, blocked action should result in anger and frustration. However, the autonomous person, getting instructions from *within,* will not experience a disabling anger, and can find acceptable ways to avoid or discharge the energies of frustration. There are available to her the traditional sublimations, alternative relationships, and perhaps even a discussion of her feelings with the man in question if that seems appropriate. While not creating high drama or ripe gossip with such a decision, people take such action every day, even though it may mean denying themselves the pleasure of genuine love feelings. Some restructure their interactions and have been known to quit their jobs. Such governance from the Center is vital and necessary, else we are at the mercy of our feelings and rationalizations, which may be insubstantial and unworthy.

It is important that the Center remain resilient and dynamic. These four systems are interlocking and dialogical, each having its own function, informing one another, and responding honestly to messages that circulate among them. It will be true that the soul-quality of the Center which integrates and sets precedents will be influenced by what goes on in the other three systems.

Reports from the air-crash victims who cannibalized the dead bodies of their comrades in order to survive clearly indicate that their action was a radical affront to their feelings and values, but reason told them the action was necessary to allow more time for the possibility of rescue. Their action was a temporary abridgement of their values; the human family must periodically examine such values if only for the sake of others who might find themselves in a similar tragic dilemma.

Occasionally in human history extremity invents action that results in new norms that set new behavioral patterns, especially in the field of medicine, where the need for information may fly in the face of belief systems and change the norms. This is illustrated in the simple process of medical post-mortems. What was thought of as "butchering the image of God" gave way to the more acceptable notion of autopsy. While the *imago Dei* might be offended by the scalpel, information for the living took precedence over the values in a theological system.

More personally, this same sort of thing may occur at the Center when one eats certain foods, takes a drink, adopts birth control, is thrown in with a member of a minority group, loses his or her virginity—all perhaps on a whim, or by accident, or as a desperate measure—and discovers a "new truth" which creates a "new value" at the Center, which in turn effects the related thoughts, feelings, and actions.

It is not possible to process the data of these four systems with their complex interactions and to measure their influence upon one another. Still, by reliable hunch, some subjective testimony, and a few "scientific observations" we know that there are many whole, autonomous persons who grow, change, and expand as persons in a world of both menace and promise.

Once, while fishing in Connecticut, I saw a boy of about fourteen line cast a small fish he had caught toward a block of gulls that hovered about his boat. A gull took the bait and immediately found itself tethered to a fishing line from which all the bird's hysterical wheeling and driving could not free it. Literally, the gull was still feeding off its environment, diving into familiar water, and climbing the air of its home. Yet everything was different. The bird was hooked—helplessly controlled by a person at the other end of a strong line. The young man played out the terrified gull, gradually subduing it, until it fell exhausted into Long Island Sound.

This is a fit analogy for what happens to many of us who refuse to take charge of our lives. The innocent gull was trapped by its ignorance and hunger, the prey of a pitiless youngster. All of the components do not fit, but the association of our life with this story is painfully clear: someone hooks us and tethers us to his or her will. Our only advantage over the poor gull is that we have more power to cut the cord. Or do we? That answer makes all the difference.

SIX MODELS **2** OF MARRIAGE

There are many ways to put marriage together, all of which may work to one degree or another. Many are distortions of what creative marriage can be, and they may be crippling to all who are connected with them, adults and children alike. In this chapter we consider some of the possibilities. There are countless others and combinations of these. It would seem helpful to get a clear image of how we do relationships. What needs get met? Are we loved or unloved? Cared about, cherished, and celebrated or lonely and in pain?

Doormat

The motto of *Doormat* marriage is "Me top dog, you underdog." This makes for a sadomasochistic alliance in which power, dominance, control, and perhaps terror are descriptive of the marriage, with one partner playing boss. Needless to say, this is a pathetic contract. These two are not equal. One is inferior, accepts a dehumanizing treatment, and surrenders autonomy. The other plays tyrant. Couples who live this way remind me of Hank and Alice who had married at age seventeen, when Alice was three months pregnant. They were thirty-nine when I first met Alice, who had spent twenty years in misery, except for the fourteen months that Hank was in Korea. Alice came to see me alone, after a fight in which Hank had left her face badly bruised and her upper lip split. She was, under normal conditions, an attractive woman. Although twelve or fifteen pounds overweight, she was clearly aware of her hair and clothes, giving them care and attention. Her blue eyes seemed sad. Her voice was husky from too many cigarettes. She reported that she had gone to family service counseling at least four times over the years for one session each time, but she would not return or was refused treatment unless her husband agreed to accompany her.

After the fight, Alice had run to Hank's sister's house three blocks away from their house, and the sister refused to take her in for the night unless she agreed to see me. She doubted that Hank would come. He had refused before. She told me that I should not telephone him. "It would only make him mad," she said. She wondered if there were something *she* could do.

"You could threaten to leave him unless he agrees to get help," I suggested.

She responded, "Oh, I could never do that. He'd kill me. That's clear. I tried to leave twelve years ago, and he came out the door after me with his rifle. Besides, the kids need their father." There were three boys, the oldest away in the navy, and other two, ages sixteen and seventeen.

"Is there anything good about living with Hank?" I asked.

"Oh my, yes! I work and have my own car. He would never hear of such a thing just three years ago. We have a nicer home than either of my sisters. And just last Christmas Hank gave me a new sewing machine. He has his good points."

"What do you two do together?" I asked.

"What do you mean?" She frowned. "You mean, like sex?"

"Well, I was really thinking of activities, parties, getting out. Recreation, things like that."

"Oh, we do lots of things together. Mostly in the summer, though. Hank likes to fish, and two years ago we got a speedboat so we could water ski, but we didn't do much of that last summer. Hank fell down the basement stairs and twisted his back." There was a pause. She stared at me, then out the window. "And as far as sex is concerned, it's okay. I never got much out of it. Hank was always too fast for me." She darted a glance at me. "You know, he comes quick."

"Did you talk about this with Hank?"

"Heavens no! I'm not that crazy. I remember once he came home and said one of the men at work told him that his wife moaned a lot when she came, and he wondered why I didn't, and I said, 'Because it doesn't *hurt.'* And Hank just laughed and laughed at that. We never mentioned it again. That must have been seven, eight years ago."

"How is it now?"

"You mean sex?" I nodded. "Tell the truth, we don't do it much any more. After his beer every night, he pretty much falls asleep, and that's it. I'm usually so tired it's just as well. Of course now and then after company or something special with our friends—a couple across the street—he'll come after me and we do it, but it doesn't take any time at all. So I don't mind occasionally."

I asked if she were satisfied with this arrangement, and raising her brows she answered, "Yeah, I guess."

I offered to see her again and she said, "What can you do for me if Hank won't come? He's funny. He might even come after you if I told him you wanted to see him." There was the slightest smile.

"What will you do?" I asked.

"Same as always, I guess. Make the best of it. What can I do? Leave? He'd find me."

"The police could help."

"How? He knows all the tricks. He'd have them eating out of his hand. He was an MP in the army. Besides, he's pretty mean sometimes. I believe he really could kill me. He knocked out our boy Tom with his bare fist once. Hit him right in the jaw."

"How about your families?"

She laughed. "They're as scared of him as I am. Besides, his father is dead. My daddy told me once when I went over there after a fight that I probably deserved it if I talked to Hank the way I used to talk to him and Mama. That was fifteen years ago. He never did anything to help. Hank's mother is in a rest home." She smiled. "There's nobody really, Doctor."

I suggested that their marriage may be a destructive game between them, as though Hank had some need to hurt her and she to suffer. To this she replied, "Oh, that's not true at all. I hope you don't think I enjoy all of this." She ran her hand across her face, lightly touching her lips.

Then I said, "All I know is that this has been going on for twenty years and everyone in your world seems helpless to stop it, and you refuse to leave him in order to give credibility to your complaints. I understand the risk in taking action against Hank, even in your coming here, but staying *there* is perhaps even more risky. And certainly nothing will change as things now stand. I would like to suggest that you begin to sort all of this out, and put together a plan of action that could be helpful for both of you. You *do* have other options."

She smiled, stood to leave, thanked me, and said, "It's no use, Doctor."

I wished her well, and suggested that she return if she wanted to. "Don't worry about me. I'll be just fine. I'm used to all this by now." She paid the fee and left. I never saw her again.

In their "doormat marriage" Alice and Hank lived in a complex system of signals, messages, hostile acts, and mock defense gestures by which they accomplished their ends. Hank hated and Alice hurt. Yet there were the goodies: house, sewing machine, her own car and job, and the fishing and water skiing. The fights seemed to be Hank's answer to his deep feelings of inadequacy, anxiety over sexual function, and hostility toward women. Alice clearly felt a need to be punished because of her guilt feelings growing out of her relationship to her parents. This is only a descriptive explanation. The day-to-day problem was that the major arenas of marriage were in shambles. They had no concept of what it meant to be friends. They were not partners: Hank "permitted" her to have certain privileges. Their love was like a battered child. Their fights were a substitute for emptiness: something was better than nothing. Even bad feelings were better than no feelings at all.

Yet contrary to popular misconceptions, this might not have been an impossible situation. The marriage might have become much more healthy and rewarding for both of them, had they been willing to work at it. Alice was not able to act, perhaps out of the *habit* of the marriage, and her need to be punished. Hank may have sensed this, and getting her *double* message ("Let's get help/No, I'm not serious"), he was not compelled to examine the relationship. Alice was not convincing. It would have taken a bold act on her part, something with clout, to get Hank's attention.

There were a number of alternatives. There could have been help from the police and the courts, especially after the evidence of their bitter fights. But Alice was not willing to press charges and move persuasively for help. Only a tragedy might have brought them to a counselor, such as a very serious problem with a son and a court order for psychiatric help.

As a counselor, I am still surprised to find how many young couples report having come from homes in which their parents regularly engaged in acrimony and/or fights. In some cases, they tell of aging parents still saying and doing cruel and destructive things to each other, with no end in sight. After a while, it becomes a way of life. The husband and wife would be lost without the ugly pain of their relationship. And these homes often give birth to those of the next generation who are also unable to function with any notion of what constitutes a healthy marriage. They never saw one.

Hank and Alice are an example of the "doormat marriage" in which male dominance and female submissiveness cooperate toward the mutual destruction of both. There are infinite variations on this theme in which people manage to control, bully, or tyrannize the spouse to the satisfaction of the negative needs and impulses in each of them.

However, it should be remembered that this matrimonial hegemony is not exclusive to the male. The reign of the "tyrant" or "boss" female in marriage is a familiar sight to counselors. The woman who "wears the pants" usually presides over her matriarchy and remains enthroned because her effete husband refuses to be his own man, contributing, insisting on his rights, making message-clear decisions, and acting with strength and conviction. Three of many capitulating male one-liners are:

1) "Whatever you say, dear."
2) "Away from the office, I'm lost."
3) "Do you know *where* my . . . ? (why my . . . ?, what my . . . ?, when my . . . ?, who my . . . ?) Every cry for help, even when camouflaged as information, can be felt by the partner as more dependency. The wife who has the answer has that much power.

If she is then given the power of *decision* and *action* in those areas, she ascends. If she is given command of all the major arenas of her husband's life, she is boss.

This third question is perhaps the most subtle of all and, of course, is seldom really *asked*. It is implied by the flaccid personality of the male: Do you know *where* my children are; *why* my dog ignores me; *what* my values, needs, dreams are; *when* I may ever do anything; *who* my friends are? The woman in charge has a "yes" for all of these and then proceeds to inform and propagandize the man. If he accepts her expertise in these matters, he is to that degree in her hands. We are not talking about mutual support and feedback, but rather the woman's systematic control of information and participation in the marriage in an effort to dominate the relationship. These women usually are demanding, loud, strong, tough, and generally officious.

More often, the ruling female is subtle and indirect, manipulating rather than plundering the man's decision and action systems. Again, we are not thinking here of the survival techniques to which women have traditionally been reduced due to the arrogance of males, but the woman who *needs* to rule the man either out of a neurotic fear or an enormous hostility, perhaps masked by the female seductress or the mama, either of which creates the "let me take care of you" atmosphere. She may come through as passive-aggressive; that is, she will not openly confront the man with an honest presentation of her feelings and ideas, but will use pouting, body complaints, denial of intercourse, etc., to get her way. Some people are even able to generate illness in order to influence their partners. This is true of both men and women.

Piggyback

 One step away from *Doormat* is *Piggyback*. The motto here is "Carry me." One partner is in a dependent relationship to the other. One makes the decisions because the other is afraid, not of the partner, but of life. The "carrier" does most of the thinking and acting in the marriage; one partner feeds off the other. *Piggyback* is a case of a psychologically crippled person getting a very expensive ride. And, of course, this is the way the taxi partners want

it; otherwise, they would change the situation. It may be the only way such persons can marry. One needs to be carried, and the other to carry. They may, however, profit from counseling.

Sally was a fifty-three-year-old nurse who came to me complaining about her husband who had become depressed after his father's death. "He sits around and does nothing. He is a good carpenter, but he's laying off work. When my daughter and her little girl come over, he goes into the bedroom and grumps. Our sex life has dropped off. He is picky and fussy about his food, and last Sunday evening he started to cry over some dumb show on TV. I've tried everything. He won't talk, play, go anywhere, or begin to think about Christmas with me. I'm scared."

She and Ed had two children, a son and a daughter, twenty-nine and twenty-seven, both divorced, and each with one child. The son was back at home, in his old room, complaining about everything, hating his job as an auto salesman when car sales had reached a new low, not dating much but out with the guys a lot. Their daughter had her own apartment, but Sally ran errands for her and often baby-sat on weekends even after a long week of nursing. The exploitive requests which the children made had no end, as Sally related incident after incident of "my children needing me."

As we talked, it became more and more clear that the entire family had been "piggybacking" on Sally for years. She had always made herself totally accessible. She even tried to anticipate their needs, writing notes or reminders, making calls, laying out clothes, leaving food prepared or cooking. She was indispensable, the Natural Nurse, the Super-Mama, feeding and comforting her world.

Ed's new and deeper dependency was about to mobilize her anger. She was beginning to resent and resist. She snapped and crackled around the house, so that the two men were asking each other in her presence, "What's with her?"

Toward the end of our first session as she paused to get her breath after a long recitation of complaints and frustrations, I asked, "And who takes care of you?" Her face went very dark and her eyes filled as she said in a softer, higher, almost childlike voice, "Nobody. Nobody ever did. Not even when I was a little girl. Do you know that I practically raised my two little brothers? Dad died when I was eight and my mother went to work, and I really became the mother to those kids. I fed and bathed them. I took them to Sunday school while Mother stayed home and slept in or cleaned house. I even rescued them from a small fire we had once. *(Pause)* And you think I got any thanks? Oh, I get cards at Christmas, but that's it. *(Pause)* You ask who takes care of me? I do. Sometimes. I guess." She had been openly crying throughout all of this. Now she was sobbing, bent over, daubing at her eyes with tissue, hurt and lonely.

As a child, Sally had learned "how to take care of," and she got most of her strokes that way. It was almost as though she was obsessively focused, both professionally and domestically, on "looking after and nursing" her world. And since she was so capable and willing, people let her. Her profession was exciting and rewarding for her, but she felt guilty about being away from the family so much; so she doubled her efforts at home, making her family even more dependent, robbing the others of their own autonomy, and getting herself left out.

There are two other important problems with this sort of relating. A person such as Sally gets most of her strokes indirectly rather than directly. That is, she feels good only if someone feels good and not because something really nice happens *to her*. It is hard to relate to this sort of person unless you come *for* something, come with an empty cup so to speak, and let them fill it for you. They spurn your approaching *them* to give or minister. *They* do the giving. Yet deep inside they are hungry and lonely.

After counseling, Sally did not break out in a dramatic confrontation with her family. She simply was less available to run errands, more direct about not having time or energy to take care of the comforts of her husband and son when they were clearly using her and not making an effort for themselves.

She used a little-girl innocence when they complained: "Oh, gee, I'm sorry I forgot to take care of that for you. Isn't it great that you were able to do it yourself?" More tartly when they angrily complained, she smiled, puckered her lips, and said "Poor babee." They began to understand. Soon she was telling them that she had plans for the evening and would not be able to get the laundry done, so perhaps she should show them how to run the machines. On one of those evenings she simply went to her bedroom and curled up with a good novel.

She loved it. She felt she was playing a game, but it seemed to her a lot more healthy. Her friends and family were getting a strong, new message from Sally. Occasionally she delayed returning routine phone calls, declined church jobs, was not always available to substitute at the hospital or baby-sit for her daughter, and turned down invitations when she felt a need to be alone. She lost weight, began going weekly to a hairdresser, and bought some new clothes.

When she told Ed that she was in therapy, he was startled. She reported it to be a "good kick in the pants" for Ed. He quit pouting and withdrawing. His depression was lifting. He began taking her out to dinner and asked her to spend the weekend with him at a new hotel near the airport.

Ed even said he would be willing to see me if she wanted him to. She told him that it was up to him to decide. A couple of days later he called in to make his own appointment. At our first session Ed decided he had some things of his own to work on.

Piggyback is a marriage game that robs both of genuine autonomy and sets up powerful dependencies. It can create the "piggy" feelings of loneliness, resentment, and of being used. While the "rider" is pampered and indulged, he or she loses power, and may even despise the babying, not knowing how to protest without hurting the partner's feelings. A few searching questions for couples are these:

If we *are* playing piggyback, who of us is which?

When do I feel like "piggy" or "rider"? Do I like the feeling? What can I do about it?

How exactly do you need me? And I you?

How well could I survive without you? And you me?

Do we *rush* to serve, protect, warn, or prepare each other?

Clutch

Clutch is about two steps away from *Doormat*. The motto here is: "Without you I would die." This couple is precariously balanced on the edge of things, holding on for dear life. It is similar to *Piggyback* except there is no clearly strong individual. Both are passive, dependent, clinging persons who pipsqueak through life, keep mostly to themselves, and are often pitifully alone even in marriage. Someone has described such a relationship this way: the rocks in his head fit the holes in hers.

Jean and Harvey were referred to me by their pastor. In response to my inquiry as to why they had come, Jean, a thin woman, poorly groomed, said, "First, we want you to know that we are decent people. What happened had nothing to do with the kind of people we are. We love each other, and we are going to be alright. We talked with our pastor, and he thought we ought to see you at least once. So we are here."

She continued telling me that she never wanted to be anything but a good wife and mother. She played the piano at the Sunday school and like to read "inspirational writers." She finished her introduction by turning to Harvey and saying, "Why don't you tell the doctor a little about you now, so he will know what kind of folks we are."

Harvey taught history at a junior college, but he admitted that he did not like his students, "who won't read, can't write, and talk too much." Out of class he mostly read, listened to the classical music station, played chess with Jean, and wrote scholarly articles about local history which were seldom published. Harvey was overweight and balding. He ushered in a neighborhood church. He said that he and Jean did not drink or smoke and seldom went to the movies because most of them were "not fit for human consumption."

There was a pause and I suggested again that they tell me why their pastor had referred them. Jean began again by describing for me their four-year-old daughter, Rebecca, "who pretty much runs things at our house." She related an embarrassing story about the child's public tantrums.

"Well, last Sunday evening I caught Harvey playing with Rebecca in the tub." She described what she had seen. She had not interrupted the sexual play, but later confronted Harvey with what she had seen. Harvey denied it. She asked him to go with her to talk with their pastor. He consented, but again denied Jean's accusation. At that point in her story I glanced at Harvey just as he broke into tears and flung himself into Jean's lap. He sobbed that he was a terrible father, who did not deserve her or Rebecca.

With this Jean began to stroke his hair and comfort him. She then pulled him up to her and rocked him like a baby. He soon sat up, told her what a wonderful wife she was, and that she should not worry, that he would never disappoint her again. They smiled longingly at each other, and Harvey turned to me to announce that they very much appreciated my help, and now would not need to return.

I tried to ask questions about what was happening. "Are you saying you do not feel a need to pursue this further?"

"I don't see why," he said, wiping his eyes. "What do you think, honey?"

"I agree," Jean answered, nodding her head.

I pushed a bit. "Wouldn't you like to explore what was going on in this incident?"

"Oh, I think I understand it," said Harvey. "I just lost control for a moment. And as I just promised Jean *(he smiled at her),* that will never happen again." He paused briefly. "You believe me, don't you, honey?"

"Certainly, I do," she said.

Again I asked, "Do you feel that what happened could in any way reflect what is going on in your marriage?"

This time Jean answered, "Why, what do you mean? We have one of the best marriages I know of. I hope you don't think we don't have good sex relations because of what happened. No, doctor, you are wrong there."

Harvey followed quickly, "We get along fine in bed. Neither of us ever had an affair, and we have a happy home."

"What about your little girl?"

He continued, "She'll be fine. We love her an awful lot and she knows it. Love and limits. That's what children need. She has the love. We just have to work on the limits a bit."

They parried all my questions and smiled through my statements of hope that they would talk with someone about all of this. Again they thanked me and left.

This is a marriage of quiet desperation. The incident with the child was another symptom of the immaturity and boredom evidenced throughout the family. They were not only poorly involved in life but also were tragically caught in the emotional webs of the marriage, as exampled by Jean's rushing quickly to the defense of their sex life, even when it was not directly under attack. There was finally an emotional confession, easy forgiveness, and a promise with automatic acceptance. It was as though "Mommie" had caught her little boy, but he was quickly reinstated into her good graces, because both saw the event as a moral issue rather than an emotional conflict. Moral issues are answered with judgment, confession, and forgiveness. Emotional issues require insearch, a look at the context in which the problem rests, causes, reasons, options, and understanding, so that behavior becomes a reasoned and rewarding thing, rather than merely "controlled."

Harvey was disenchanted with his vocation. Jean appeared satisfied with her life as wife and mother; yet both husband and daughter (with her tantrums) were acting out. To enrich this marriage and family would have required considerable work; yet there are indications that, with courage, Harvey and Jean could grow. The marriage seems tight, fixed, simplistic, and uninspired, caught in routine and perhaps doomed to more incestuous incidents in quest of any kind of "turn-on." While not a picture of hope, such a marriage is not necessarily terminally ill if the couple can heed the symptoms and get help.

Idol

The motto is "Worship me." One partner considers himself or herself to be worthy of very special attention. The "superperson" wants lots of praise for beauty, talent, brains, money, whatever. The other can only stand in awe, shrink in public, and lead the ovation with friends. It is a tiresome marriage. Most often it is the wife who worships. She begins every social event with a "Guess what my marvelous husband has done now?" sort of invitation. You're a good friend according to how extravagantly you guess: "A $10,000 raise?", "Promoted to president?", "He's jogging!"

Idol is another form of slavery. The spouse who insists on being idolized is probably suffering from narcissism. Narcissus, in Greek mythology, was a handsome young man who fell in love with his own reflection in a pool and pined away until he fell in and drowned. In a marriage in which there is the worshiped and the worshiper, the first insists on a special privilege, deference, and inordinate expressions of gratitude and adoration. The other feels fortunate to be able to participate in such a marriage. For the worshiping partner, it is a great "honor" to serve and share the limelight with this marvelous mate.

Lloyd and Jackie were in their early thirties and had been married five years. They made a handsome couple. He was an airline executive, and she had been a hostess when Lloyd met and married her. He insisted that she quit work and keep their townhouse, "stay in shape" with a spa membership, and generally run errands for him and his horses. Most of his free time was spent caring for, training, and showing horses. Jackie was allowed to do very little directly for the horses, nor could she ride them. She was forbidden to buy her own horse. Lloyd did not want any but purebreds, and they were too expensive simply for Jackie's pleasure. She continued to assist him and sacrificed her own desire for a horse. She suggested finally that she be allowed to get a riding horse and keep it at another stable. Lloyd was put out. It was *his* hobby, his very serious hobby. He did not want to be distracted from blood horses, and he did not want her energy for his hobby going elsewhere. He did not suggest any solution except to say, "Why can't you just enjoy what I am doing with horses?" Most of their money went into his hobby.

When Jackie came for her first appointment, she complained of migraine headaches, feeling jittery, not being able to sleep, and worrying her mother with all the Valium she was taking. "I never feel like eating," she said, "although I do find myself into cookies or chips sometimes before I even realize what I'm doing. But with Lloyd the way he is, I could never allow myself to gain weight." She laughed. "I think he'd divorce me over five pounds in the wrong places."

"What do you do when you can't sleep?" I asked.

"Well, let's see. Last night I got up and sewed. I'm making Lloyd's shirt for the show. He looks so great up there on that big horse. You can almost hear the women 'ooh' and 'aah' when he rides out." She laughed nervously. "I really expect them to swoon. He said one did last time, but I didn't see it. I dunno. Maybe. He's beautiful."

"What about you, Jackie? Where do you see things going for you?" I queried.

"Me? Wherever Lloyd goes, I guess. Doing things for him. He calls me his maidservant. 'Hey, maidservant,' he'll say, 'get me my watcha-ma-call-it.' And I go flying. It's really a sort of honor for me to be on his team. Then it's show time, and he's out there riding, looking like a god, and I say under my breath, 'He's mine, all mine, girls. So hands off.'" She was visibly excited.

"What's he like otherwise?" I inquired. "You know, away from the horses, just around the house?"

"Oh, there. Well, he's rather a loner. Of course, he's at the stables a lot—or on the phone, or going to see someone about horses. He exercises, swims, keeps himself in perfect condition. No hobbies but horses. He reads books and magazines about horses, mostly just before bed. He even reads fiction about horses."

"Okay. But what about you? What are you doing all this time?"

"Oh, things. Cleaning house, laundry, food. Lloyd likes good food, special dishes. I sew. I've learned to make all his show outfits. And they are gorgeous. Lloyd says it's the best thing I do. It would cost a fortune to buy what I can make. That's how it started. My mother sews, and I never sewed a thing until once she suggested I do it when I told her how much Lloyd wanted a certain jacket that sold for $200. A hand-stitched thing, embroidery, the works. My mother and I made it. Well, I helped *her*. But now I do it all. Anyway, I gave it to him for his birthday that year, and did he ever love it!"

I leaned forward. "Okay, now *you*. Tell me about *you*. Are you only Lloyd's maidservant?"

She laughed. "Oh, goodness, no. I read nights mostly. Watch a little TV when Lloyd is busy. Visit my mom. Recently I've gotten into plants some, too."

"Do you have your own friends?"

"Oh, yeah, sure. There are a couple of other girls whose husbands are also into horses. I see them sometimes—lunch, a movie. I went to the Chinese exhibition with Vi. Mostly I see the girls when we go out of town to do a show. We all go together, three couples. We get a bunch of rooms at a motel. We have fun drinking and dancing after the show, unless Lloyd wants to get to bed so we can hit the road early for home."

Her whole life was Lloyd and the horses. I could not find her outside her servitude. "What did you want to do before you met Lloyd?" I asked.

"Fly. I always wanted to fly—since I was little. I mean really little, like four or five."

"And how long were you a hostess?"

"Four years."

"Will you ever go back to that?"

"I doubt it. Why should I?"

"But you wanted that for so long!"

"Oh, yes. But that was 'BL,' before Lloyd." She smiled. There was a pause.

"Will you have a family? Do you want children?"

"I do. Lloyd doesn't. At least I thought I did. The more I see and hear about kids, the more I think I'm glad my man doesn't want any. Lloyd said just the other day that a poll showed that couples without kids were happier than those with them."

The session closed with my asking if she thought Lloyd would come in to see me. She said she thought he might. Her mother had advised her to see me when she told her about her body complaints. She would ask Lloyd that night and let me know. She said she felt better and wanted to make another appointment for herself for later that same week.

The next morning my secretary said that her husband had called in and canceled Jackie's appointment. When my secretary asked if she might give me the reason for the cancellation, he said he thought his chiropractor could handle the situation faster and cheaper.

Two months later Jackie was back in my office on her mother's arm. Lloyd was furious and had ordered her to file for divorce if she returned to see me. After a year of hard work and the divorce, Jackie was a different person and considering nursing school. She still wanted to serve, but she had a deeper understanding of her own emotional needs, greater self-esteem and autonomy, and clearer personal goals that were hers for *her* life.

Over the years of my practice there have been many similar marital arrangements:

There was the man whose mother was killed in an auto accident when he was six. His father remarried, and his second mother died of cancer when he was fifteen. He was married when he was twenty-seven to a woman eight years his senior, with two small children. He became her "third child" and he shamelessly worshiped her. The problem was that she came to resent his "weakness and baby talk" and the fact that she was responsible for the business and recreation of the entire family. By the time they came to me, she was involved in an affair, which he knew about. He told her that he was able to handle it if she needed that. Privately to me he said, "I can't let a little thing like an affair spoil our marriage. She'll be back. She did the last time. This is one fantastic woman. I guess she could do about anything she wants, and I don't think I would really object. She is wise and fair, and she would not be doing this if there were not some deep need." They were finally divorced, and he moved in with his father, where he has remained unmarried, and without therapy. It is very hard for a mate to feel like an adult spouse in a peer relationship when she feels like the only grown-up in the house.

An older couple came to see me after thirty-seven years of his worshiping her. They finally hit a snag when she wanted him to retire at sixty, from work that he deeply enjoyed, and move to California to be near their daughter. She said, "Why is it that you have to be so stubborn after all these years?" Privately he shared a letter with me which he had received from his daughter, who said she and her husband did not want her mother living nearby. The letter concluded with: "You, of all people, should know how mother is—always right, demanding attention. She thinks she's the Virgin Mary. Do whatever you have to, Daddy, but keep her there. If you don't, I swear that Phil and I will move to Australia." After a number of sessions, the worshiping husband turned agnostic. He and his daughter confronted his wife, who decided that being loved was better than being worshiped.

Hide-and-Seek

 The motto is: "Where are you?" The spouse here tries to keep the mate guessing. She or he is a mystery: busy, hidden, vague, and always somehow not quite satisfied with the spouse. The partner never knows where he or she stands, feels off-balance, with the other perhaps subtly threatening to "lower the boom" if the partner is not careful. And on top of it all, the seeking spouse is encouraged to "try to understand how I feel" and asked, "Why do you say that I avoid you?" This is followed by, "I don't know why you seem to find me difficult and strange. The folks at the office think I'm okay. *They* like me!"

Geri and Tom had been married almost sixteen years when Geri came to see me. She was a tall, slim woman and an attractive mother of two teenage girls. Her deferring nature was immediately apparent as we met: "I know you are a very busy man, and I am sorry to take your time. Besides, I doubt you or anyone can tell me what to do about my situation. Anyway, it's been going on for so long; I wonder if we could change it if we tried."

She paused for a quick, tight smile and a long sigh. "My mother says I am lucky to have him. Tom. That he is a better man than my father was. He's dead. And I should just look around at my neighbors. One is divorced, and another deserted. Even our minister is leaving his wife, I think. *(Pause)* It really is me, I guess. At least Mother and Tom and the girls seem to think so. They laugh at me. Tom says it's a wonder sometimes he comes home at all. *(Pause)* Sometimes I feel I am being ignored. I ask them to do something and it gets *half* done. Come to think of it, everything in my life seems half done. We never did really finish off the basement. Kids played in it when they were little but we never use it now. And it's all that way. Half done. I'm the only one that goes to church anymore. Tom never did except on special days, or when the girls were doing something they wanted him to attend. Half done. That's really funny. Dishes, beds, washing, lessons. Even our sex life. I never thought of it before. Tom and I never enjoy it *together*. We aren't lovers. It's as though one night it's for him and another night it's for me, according to how we feel. Who's tired, or whatever."

She laughed. Amused and with the charm of a child who has made a discovery, she said, "Yep. I have a half-baked life alright." The laugh was now more cynical. "And guess who does the other half, the half they leave, the part they hate?" There was a long pause as she looked away, staring.

"Does Tom help?" I ventured.

"Tom? *Him?* Heaven's no! But then, why should he? He works hard and provides quite well for us." She looked back at me.

"You want to tell me about Tom?"

"I'll be glad to. He's forty-one, tall, dark, and handsome. Very athletic. Does not drink or smoke. Loves foreign cars. Owns his own piano, and has been top banana in his agency for the past six years, and among the top in the whole nation. He's great. No doubt about it. He is courteous, thoughtful, and generous. A good scout. Last year for my birthday he sent me to Hawaii to see my brother." She paused again and her eyes filled. "It's just that he is gone *all the time*. He's in an auto club, a flying club, and of course there is all the stuff that goes on at his tennis club. He has breakfast meetings, plays handball at lunch, swims one night a week, and mixes in golf and tennis in good weather. Plus, of course, there are all the local teams and their games. Late nights he reads reports and things. And all this after many nights of two or three appointments. He can mix work and play better than any one I know."

"Would you say that even his play sounds like work?" I asked.

"Well, maybe," she answered. "But he seems to love it all. And the girls are just as bad. Kim is in everything at school. Every group she's in is always calling to find her. *(She laughed.)* And she's always somewhere else. Sue's the senior. Has her own car and is a nurse's aide after school. She wants to be a nurse. But I never see her either. She has this great dating life going and says she'll never marry. I don't know. They're all so busy. Is that good?" I raised my brow. She smiled sadly.

"What about you?" I asked.

"Me? Well, there's the trouble. I don't have the energy they do. I just can't keep up. I had rheumatic fever when I was eight and I've never been the same. Even when the girls were tiny, they exhausted me. Doctors say I am fine. No scars on the heart or anything. *(She laughed.)* But *I* say I have never been the same. *(Pause)* Tom agrees. He says I'm not as strong even as when we married. I was twenty then. Of course he was always doing things I couldn't. Swimming, biking, skating. We did dance a little, but I tired so quickly. But I do *try*. We are members of a dinner club, and we go there faithfully, every first Saturday night. I enjoy that if we leave early enough. It's hard to tear Tom away before midnight. I turn into a pumpkin at midnight."

"You mentioned the choir."

"Oh, yes. I do that, but I'm the quietest little soprano there. After a special choir program, like the Christmas cantata, I'm exhausted."

"What else do you and Tom do?"

"Not much actually. *(Pause)* We almost never have sex anymore. I guess that's what got me here today. He complains. I'm too skinny, too whiney, too slow. Too something. Or he's tired. That's a switch, isn't it? The guy tired. *(Pause)* But it used to be good. *(She smiled.)*

Well, pretty good. I was never a Mata Hari. I still like to lie close to him though. Sometimes he lets me scratch his back until he goes to sleep. Sometimes I just lie there and watch him sleep. Guess I am just hungry for the sight of him." She laughed and her eyes filled.

"What does the laugh say?"

She was embarrassed. "Oh, I don't know. It sounded silly to say I was hungry for the sight of a man who was lying there asleep on his stomach with his face to the wall."

She had talked for some time, and I sensed it could go on forever with all of her complaints falling flat as she laughed at her needs and put herself down with quotes from Mother, Tom, and the girls. So I gave her a note pad and asked her to draw a picture of the way she felt about her life. After the usual jokes about not being an artist, she became quiet and closed her eyes to get the picture. In a few moments tears began again. She opened her eyes and, blotting them with a Kleenex, began to draw.

She explained her drawing. "That's me—up a tree. The bear is my fears. I'm scared. Tom and the girls are in the jet flying away and leaving me out on a limb over a cliff." She was very clear about her condition.

In subsequent sessions we spent time working on Geri's self-image. After a complete physical examination, she was told that she was in excellent health, except for her weight, which was too light, and could exercise as she chose. Soon she joined a therapy group and was supported in an expanding program of self-enhancing activities. She changed her hairstyle and grooming, began reading and watching programs on the public television station, and started a course in guitar. Since she did not work out of the home, she began attending a variety of programs in the city.

She confronted her family more. When things were half done, they were told to redo them. She asked Tom about having the basement completed so they could use it to entertain. He put her off. So she called three companies in town for estimates. Tom then took time to plan with her, ordered materials, and the two of them went to work on the basement. She began giving small dinner parties with two other couples, and Tom was there in his own inimitable style as host. She put together her own little crash "Eliza Doolittle Program." There was no heavy, torturous therapy—just a decision to risk some things. The depression lifted as she liked herself better.

By this time the family knew she was up to something. They believed she was just going to "another church meeting" when she came to the group. The family hardly missed her. But they knew she was different. She said she was praying harder. Actually she was doing that, too.

Then in the spring, Tom won a trip to Miami and he asked her to go along. This time she did. Before, she would have used the excuse that the girls needed her, and Tom would have agreed. They had a great time together. She reported to the group: "Good food. I gained three pounds. Good fun. And good sex." She was getting into Tom's world as much as possible, and he began to participate in hers. She then asked for her own sports car. Tom was surprised, then angry, and finally amused. "Nothing fancy," she said, "just a small, yellow Audi Fox." She got it, and Tom spent an entire weekend with her, giving her pointers, while she did the driving. "After my old klunker," she said, "this little beauty is enough to make a gal leave home."

Things were better than Geri could ever remember them. The girls still went their own way, but they helped more and took her more seriously. "Actually, I'm sort of glad they're growing away from us. I want to concentrate on Tom," she said. When she asserted herself, the girls just stared at her, shook their heads, and did as she asked. Geri was even able to remind her mother that she was not a child and Mother might very well learn to keep some of her opinions to herself. Mother did not telephone for two full days; then she called to say, "You've changed, and I don't like it. Are you going to those liberation meetings?"

The marriage really began to move, however, when Geri announced to Tom that she was enrolled in a flying course and expected to be able to "have the family plane for heavy dates." She had thought to surprise him one day at the airport by offering to pilot the plane on one of their trips but decided that was "too cutesy."

Soon afterwards Geri left the group. She was becoming a beautiful, strong, autonomous woman, who was doing her life with a lot of satisfaction. Also, she and Tom were friends, talking and sharing. Their partnership was one of equals, with a contract that Geri would not take a job. She said, with a slight, becoming arrogance, "I'm too busy."

She had accepted volunteer jobs at her church and the art gallery. She and Tom were lovers. Their sex life was much improved. She was teasing Tom about getting a vasectomy.

It sounds like a fairy tale, too good to be true. Actually, it was even better than this account can suggest. Once Geri decided that *she* was her problem and began to take herself seriously in every way, she was able to reconstruct her marriage. Confronting Tom would have been calamitous. She had been dull and complaining. She had been afraid. She had *needed* them. They did not *need* her as she was prepared to be needed, but they used her because Mommie was all she offered. In fact, she was a drag. Her own growth was personal and permanent. She was marvelous to watch. Everyone felt the impact of the shy, tired female becoming a head-up, happy woman. I never met Tom. She wanted it that way.

Seesaw

 This is a face-to-face relationship, observed and observing. There is closeness with distance; the gap can be closed for deeper intimacy. I can recall standing up with my partner on a seesaw, holding hands across the fulcrum, and with a little knee action having a few moments of fun until we fell. The seesaw model suggests an interesting aspect of a dialogical relationship. It is an interdependent model. Each needs the other in order to seesaw. Yet, one has the good feeling of carrying his or her own weight, lifting, then waiting, rising and falling in an undulating rhythm, responsive and responsible. It is even possible to "coast" for a while, feet up, eyes closed, while the watchful partner provides the energy and monitors the rhythm, "taking care of" the other. Every analogy finally breaks down. So does the seesaw. Yet it comes closer than most to suggesting many of the mutual and reciprocal elements of a healthy marriage. We shall attempt in the following chapters to set forth what appear to be the necessary elements of the seesaw model of marriage between autonomous adults.

Before you proceed, it may be helpful to create your own model. Perhaps it is at first only a simple cartoon like Geri's as a way of getting at what it feels like to be in your marriage. Often it is useful to model in order to uncover buried feelings and attitudes. Once a group of couples used boxes of Tinker-Toys to build models of their marriages. Some worked together, others apart. Some argued and struggled over favorite pieces. One man took over and built while his wife passively watched. Another pouted and withdrew when his wife accused him of being "too slow and unimaginative." The process was illuminating. The feelings flowed. All agreed that the exercise was in some poignant ways reflective of things that went on in their marriage. Take a few minutes to get a mental picture of how you feel about your marriage. Now draw a picture of it. If you can, share it with your mate. Invite him or her to draw a picture also and discuss the pictures. How do they make you feel about life together?

THE FRIENDSHIP *3*
OF MARRIAGE

Friendship is the foundation of adult marriage. When two people find each other in this world of so many chance meetings, when they risk disclosing themselves, come to care deeply about one another in all the when, where, how, and why of life and make a living thing of closeness, we have an impressive event. If they go deeper to confront one another with their closeness, believing in the survival of their love though it be driven to the wall, we have a miracle. But when that man and woman create a friendship together and add, "I want to spend my life with you," we have something more impressive than any miracle. We have the first phase of perhaps the greatest drama of the human saga, in which most of all that it means to be man and woman is searched and tested, tried and celebrated, in anguish and joy. If this sounds utopian, visionary, and like nothing you ever see, it is still worth watching for and working for in our lonely time.

The Need to Know and Be Known

Definitions of the healthy personality often include lists and descriptions of what may be called basic human needs. One need badly overlooked is the *need to be known* as one characteristic of the mature adult. We see that need expressed everywhere. It is the first ingredient of friendship—the beginning of any significant relationship.

A friend visits a club or church, is ignored, and complains, "No one even knew I was there." He was not acknowledged as being present, the first step in knowing.

A teenager erupts at a negligent parent, "I'm your daughter, but you don't know me at all. You don't know anything about me. You barely know my name."

Creation begins in the Bible with naming: heaven, earth, waters, darkness, light, evening and morning, and the first day. All are given names: Adam, Eve, animals, birds, and plants. Infants learn to name: Dada, Mama. Naming is the first act of language, and perhaps the deepest sense of knowing. Little children make the connection. The five-year-old daughter of our friends joyfully declared to her parents after her baptism: "Now God knows my name." The ritual represented a special moment of recognition.

The Hebrew language uses the same word for knowing with the mind and the sexual experiencing of another person in intercourse. *To know* suggests a profound awareness of another with a depth and intimacy that is extraordinary.

A couple said to me, "We lived on that street for almost two years, and never really got to know anybody there. Oh, we spoke when we went out to get the paper, and once when everybody came out to watch firemen get a cat out of the tree. But getting to know people takes effort."

A man once told me, "I want to smoke the biggest cigar and drive the biggest car this side of the Anacostia river. I want people to know who I am."

Eric Berne, inventor of Transactional Analysis, has a book entitled *What Do You Say After You Say Hello?* "Hello" is the first step in the hazardous and miraculous movement toward intimacy, toward being deeply known by another. A friendship begins with a need to be known. Perhaps this even somehow precedes the need to be loved;

certainly chronologically and in fact it must. But in some ways the need to be known by another may be the primary psychological and social need.

We do not have to argue for the primacy of the need to be known over the need to be loved. We are reminded that it is not possible to be loved until we are known. Becoming known is simply a necessary step toward becoming loved. Be that as it may, even when we are loved, and when we do not expect the whole sequence of known-to-loved to develop in a new relationship, we still enjoy being known. We like to be introduced and have someone say with obvious delight, "Oh, I know who you are."

Many of the emotional conflicts that we find in people have to do with the *fear* of being known. If you know me, you can control me. If you know me, you may find that I am bad or stupid or empty— whatever my fear. If you know me, you will know my weakness, and you will hurt me. If I let you know me, then I feel obligated to get to know you, and then I am committed to a relationship which frightens me.

Some years ago, J. William Pfieffer and John E. Jones gave us the "Joharie" window in the their book, *A Handbook of Structured Experiences for Human Relations Training*. It looks like this:

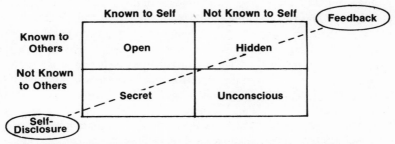

In quadrant one we have the *open* area of the person, those things clearly available, known to self and to others, and as obvious as size, color of hair and eyes—that which is apparent.

In quadrant two is the *hidden* aspect, self, which is called the "bad breath" area. Robert Burns spoke of this area when he suggested what a gift it would be if we could see ourselves as others see us.

In quadrant three are the *secrets,* that which we cover and protect:

bits of history, our fears and failures, dreams and loves, things we are shy about revealing or are ashamed of, or even things which give us a secret delight.

In quadrant four are all the elements of the *unconscious,* buried by time or will, locked out of awareness. It is this part of the self that Freud and others have uncovered with hypnosis, free association, dreams, fantasies, jokes, and slips of the tongue. It is a fascinating underworld of all sorts of materials. Freud thought the unconscious contained mostly the ugly and unhappy personal experiences which the conscious mind declined to hold and thus buried. Carl Jung said that there are also some good things there, symbols of the entire human experience.

It would appear, then, that the unconscious is both a private and a human-family collection of historical fragments, symbols (fire, rainbow), myths (generation, salvation stories), archetypes (Mother, Father, Hero), intuitions, fantasies, energies, and dreams forgotten. It is like a computer, seemingly able to summon almost any combination of words, sounds, feelings, action, and vision that the mind can contain and flash them across the screen of the mind with terror or delight, in dream or fantasy, to inform or obscure reality. It was Elias Howe's dream of a knight snatching a lady's scarf and threading it through the eye in the point of his lance that gave him the idea of the sewing machine needle, which pushes rather than pulls the thread through the cloth. Some believe that it is in the unconscious that the ultimate direction of one's life is day by day being determined—below the level of consciousness, where a profound and subtle mixing and sorting of one's total experience is constantly occurring, winsomely or tyrannically to lead us down the paths of our destiny.

The process of *becoming known* by another is dialogical. It occurs in the interpersonal exchange of impressions, ideas, feelings, etc., as people get acquainted. In the second quadrant of the window, it may be *seen* by another that my jacket is torn or that I ignored a red traffic light, neither of which I realized until someone who cared was willing to tell me. In the third quadrant I *became* known as I disclosed that my favorite cake is German chocolate; that it annoyed me to have my wife tell me I missed the traffic signal; and that I prefer playing baseball to watching the game. In the fourth quadrant I am revealed in the telling of a dream or fantasy, in a slip of the tongue, or in a painting of mine that a friend interprets.

We become known in all four quadrants. The dialogue is the process of self-disclosure and feedback suggested by the broken diagonal line connecting "self-disclosure" and "feedback" in the diagram. It is in this process that a relationship grows in what Martin Buber refers to as the in-betweenness of the I-Thou experience. The ability to self-disclose and handle feedback freely and appropriately with another, so that an in-betweenness emerges in which understanding, respect, and affection can flourish, is an essential mark of emotional health and maturity.

It is in this dialogue that communication occurs. To communicate is to *talk* and *touch*. We may also whistle, wink, frown, draw pictures, or rely on ESP. Even body language is itself a language, and hence a kind of talk. In Transactional Analysis we speak of giving someone positive or negative *strokes,* so that even touching is talking and vice versa. It may very well be that the most reassuring touch of all is a warm hug, and the deepest word to be communicated is "closeness."

If we have a reciprocal need to be known and this gives pleasure, we will take special care that our need and pleasure are satisfied by creating a mutual closeness. However, if our need and pleasure transcend all other needs, we may sacrifice honesty and our integrity in order to get closeness. It is then that trust is jeopardized. If both parties withhold truth for the sake of closeness, the relationship will last only as long as neither party has a greater need for truth than for closeness.

The Need to Trust and Be Trusted

In a healthy friendship there is a *need to trust* and to be trusted. In the disclose/feedback movement toward closeness, a need to trust is paramount. We must be certain that the message between us is authentic and understood. As the dialogue expands from the first *Hello,* trust begins to form from words, body expressions, and the reasonableness of our story. We *tell ourselves* with a cluster of signals, trusting the receiver to be open and fair, not expecting *double proof:* that is, not only to prove *my* credibility, but also to *disprove* the other's prejudice or hang-up about *all* men, *all* women, *all* psychologists, etc. It is the *double-proof* syndrome that often sabotages relationships at the outset. For trust to develop, we must be able to *check it out* (by raising questions in order to verify our assumptions or feelings) as well as to give *feedback.*

Jim and Sue are concluding dinner together a week after they met.

JIM: "You know, I think it takes a lot of courage to be able to come right out and tell me that you are seeing a psychologist."

SUE: "Really?" *(Here we go again. He thinks I'm nuts.)*

JIM: "Yeah. I don't think most people would. I wouldn't. At least not on the first date."

SUE: "Why not? There's nothing to be ashamed of." *(On which date would he like to be told? Number two, number nineteen?)*

JIM: "Oh, I didn't mean to imply that there is. I guess I just feel it takes guts to admit to it on the first date. It's not like I'm a total stranger, but you hardly know me, and . . ."

SUE: "Look! Cut it, will you? I *know* how you feel. You've certainly made that clear. I'm sorry I even brought the subject up. You obviously feel that anyone who goes to a shrink is crazy. For your information, I started therapy to find out why I get involved with weak, dependent men who drink too much. And after seeing you inhale those two martinis before dinner, it looks as though my choice has not improved. Why don't you just take me home right now!"

The first hazard is building trust in the double-proof washout. Here Sue not only requires that Jim *sound believable,* but he must also carefully avoid the innuendo and allusion that fits her own *stereotype.* Had she not been so defensive, she might have *checked out* why he felt she had courage, rather than assuming that he was implying that therapy is such an awful thing that its disclosure should be saved till later in the relationship.

It might have gone this way with a little more care on Sue's part.

JIM: "You know, I think it takes a lot of guts for you to be able to just come right out and tell me that you are seeing a shrink."

SUE: "Really? Why do you say that?"

JIM: "Oh, I don't know. I just don't think most people would. I wouldn't. At least not on the first date."

SUE *(smiling):* "Well, on which date would you prefer I tell you?"

JIM *(laughing):* "Oh, I didn't mean it that way. I just think it's really neat that you are so open. I don't let people in like that. I wish I could. They say I am hard to get to know. You think that's true?"

SUE: "Well, I don't know. From what you just said I think you are doing very well letting me know how you see yourself. You seem to feel you are stand-offish, and it seems that some people have confirmed that. You're letting *me* in."

JIM: "Thanks. That's really nice. You know, it really is easy to talk with you. Gee, I don't know, maybe I *would* have told you on the first date that I was seeing a shrink."

Both are laughing.

The first dialogue was actually reported to me by the woman who told Jim off and later regretted her response. She herself role-played the second dialogue in my office. After role play she said, "I was more eager to prove him a bastard than to understand him, and I turned out to be a bitch instead."

She asked Jim to share a coffee break with her and checked out her role play by asking with a smile, "What were you *really* trying to say to me the other night before I jumped on you?" His response was remarkably what she had put together in her fantasy. She came back pleased that she, at least, had been able to fantasize the healthier dialogue.

Trust is built like a New England stone wall. The base is dug in and the stones are *fitted* stone upon stone, great ones and small ones, each in what seems to be its own, special place, so that mortar is not even necessary in order for the wall to stand. There is self-disclosure and feedback, no double proofing; check it out and make the circle: another stone in place. Slowly but surely more and more is trusted to the other. We become trusted and trusting.

The Need to Accept and Be Accepted

Carl Rogers speaks of a counselor having *unconditional positive regard* for his client if there is to be rapport between them. To be accepted is to be seen as a person of worth, to be treated as one who does not have to prove that she or he is of value. A husband once said to his wife, "I will love you when you lose weight." She replied, "When you love me, I will lose weight." Neither felt accepted simply for who he or she was. Each felt unacceptable to the other. He was really saying, "If you loved me, you would lose weight." And she was saying, "And if you really loved me, the weight would not matter that much to us and I would lose it." One's patience can be pressed beyond the breaking point, but there is some truth in what each is saying. It is almost as though they have set up the problem to see what the *limits of acceptance* are. Should the wife take the six-month reducing program alone? Should the husband grit his teeth and give her the talking-touching love she says she must have if she is to lose weight?

The problem goes much deeper. Acceptance has to do with the way we make each other *feel*. The wife did not *feel* accepted by her husband. She felt inadequate as wife, mother, and his mate among his friends. Her laugh was loud and nervous. Her ideas faded quickly. Her feelings were unclear, her opinions equivocating, her gossip malicious. She was unsure of herself. He did nothing to reassure and support, but merely let her hang there and get fat, and left her in her misery by blaming her extra twenty pounds for his rejection.

To build acceptance, it would be necessary for him to affirm his desire to be close to her by accepting the present weight condition, which he had helped to create, and moving close enough to her for her to put together a contract with him. The weight is just a symptom. He would need to say something like this: "I care about you. I have no need to hurt or neglect you. I want you to feel that I not only love you, but also I accept you as you are right now. I am glad you are in my world. I have the feeling that I sometimes make you feel insecure, and I want you to talk with me about those feelings, so together we can do something to change them. I want *both* of us to accept you."

Acceptance does not mean that, no matter what, I accept you and your condition. It is not a "your mate, love me or leave me" situation. It is not fair to ask that our mate simply tolerate whatever condition we present. Acceptance says: "I understand where you are, and I trust your goodwill to do something about the situation. I will support you in every healthy way possible while you work on the situation. Wherever I can help, I will. Trust me, and be sure to tell me how you need me."

Acceptance says that I am prepared to let you be who you are, and at the same time feed back to you how you make me feel. I will do this as honestly and gently as I can. I trust you to be open to my feelings and help me to communicate to you in the most constructive way possible. Little things help. For example, tell me when I am too quick to criticize, when it is the wrong time or place, or when you feel that I am unfair. Trust the process. If each wants acceptance, yet each needs the mirror of the other, we must be honest and open, believing that we can both grow toward becoming the persons we want to be for ourselves and one another.

The Need to Like and Be Liked

To know, trust, accept, and *like* another brings us to the first clear sign of love in our movement toward genuine intimacy in adult marriage.

To like someone is different from loving. To like means to take pleasure in, to enjoy, to feel good in another's presence. When apart, we feel the distance, miss the other, and desire reunion. We say, "It is so good just to hear your voice," by phone when apart. Upon reunion, it may be, "Let me look at you."

Most friendships are *about* something: ideas, people, things, games, activities. Some people are just fun to be with. We seek them out, curious to find out what they are doing now. They amuse us, add zest. We *like* them. They seem to like us. "No big deal, no heavy trip."

Somehow, it seems important in friendship to know *where the action is* with each other, where the energy is flowing, what has your best attention, where your life is focused. We have these kinds of friendships, and know what they are about, how they feed us. It is also a creative thing to do in marriage, to have exchanges in which we share the exciting centers of our lives as they keep emerging. This is not to displace other friendships. But a flat, dull *friendship* is an anomaly and can be disastrous to a healthy marriage. It is hard to *like* in a relationship that is a drag.

We usually *like* those who give us good feelings. We take delight in them. We want to be close to them. We feel comfortable with them. There is the lightness of humor and spoofing. A *guess what* spirit animates meetings: guess what I did, read, heard, saw. *Guess who* can be fun, if it does not degenerate into vicious gossip. We need to bring something to the meeting of friends. We bring *ourselves,* but that sounds a bit pretentious and abstract. People are also about *something.* The style, content, and feeling of sharing what we are about is what gets the "I *really* like being with you" sort of exchange flowing.

If the relationship is reciprocal, *connections* are created (I'm glad you feel that way too; we seem to know a lot of the same people; let's get together again some time soon), *bonds* are established (you really make me feel good; I'm sure glad you are around today; I need to see you right away), and *expectations* exchanged (I knew I could count on you; you were the first one I wanted to see; the nicest thing about London will be that you are there). All these feelings need not die in marriage. They are always available in all of us, with somebody, for somebody.

There are times when "I like you" carries even deeper feelings of that moment than if the person should say "I love you." There is a celebrative spirit, a *joie de vivre* in the enthusiastic "I like you" that confirms the moment and links the persons as little else does. The *liking side* of marriage is analogous to the resonance of a good violin. No matter how accurate the notes, the music does not get out; it does not go anywhere, unless the body of the instrument speaks. Married couples need to like each other. When you really think about it, why should people want to be married at all if they do not like each other?

The Need to Share

I recall once leaving in the middle of a film because the woman I most wanted to *share* it with me could not be there. It was a powerful, moving story, which for me at that time spoke to our relationship, and I could not handle the feelings of the movie, which I knew I would need to discuss, if she could not experience them with me. We returned to the movie together a week later, and I was glad I had waited.

Dear Dian:

Sharing with you is one of the most intimate experiences of my life. We have discussed almost everything so far. And I do not feel diminished, as some have told me they do. Rather, I feel clearer, stronger, richer. At first we were threatened by the things we each needed to say. So we shared our feelings about that, and I guess we decided that if we could not discuss the hard things, what *would* we be sharing in this marriage? No one is a fully *disclosed* person, but having you at the end of the day to share deeply in my life helps to keep the *mystery of us* alive, helps to make the magic of meeting a time to await and cherish. And when you open your day to me, I recall the moment as a little boy when I climbed a few feet into a great tree and peered for the first time into a bluejay's nest of small greenish, speckled eggs. I am glad that we decided long ago to share with each other in a warm ritual of daily meeting.

We have shared our *gods,* the men and women who have ennobled our lives with their ideas and creations: the philosopher and artist, musician and painter, parent and friend, teacher and mentor, the feeling and doing people who called us to be who we were at a time and place of revelation, when the path turned upward toward the mountain, downward into the valley, beside the clear stream, beyond the wall. We have shared all. Or at least all that mattered. Also, we have hung back and waited for the other to emerge from dark encounters and said, "You made it. I knew you would. I could only wait." You were there. You are here. I am glad.

We have shared our *dreams,* the fantasies left over from childhood, the broad-scoped visions of how life might be fashioned, and the drab whims of our poverty or fatigue that fester out of the wouldn't-it-be-nice-if-once-before-we-die quarrels with life's knuckle sandwich. We have dreamed together: "Then what will we do?" We have pricked each other's bubble: "And if you got it, what would you do with it?" We have even demanded dreams when it seemed there were only nightmares: "You're a drag. Look around. There's water in Missouri. Let's buy a little sailboat. The roses are blooming in Loose Park. Write me a poem. If you want that degree, we'll find a way to get to Chicago . . . all five of us, all five of us."

We have shared our *grief:* your father, my mother; both dead. We knew they really loved us, and so we celebrated them, even in their passing. The other tears: Korea, the tortured letters and the stupid, shortwave phone call from Tokyo, and Jenny, a year old before I saw her; the theological trip, Baptist and Unitarian (What shall we teach our children?), the joyous devotional watch we kept in Groton and Storrs, only to leave sightless from Seminary Hill, weeping through the prayer-poems; the late night vigils with our three children needing to escape us into the world. And so much more. This is grief? Readers will complain that ours was nothing. But it was ours, and it got us in the gut. And who is to say among the mourners which heart is heaviest? You carry what you must, and if it is more than before, you may cry out among the saddest, and who will say it is nothing?

We have shared our *guilt*, nothing too heavy, mind you. No great schism of the soul or body. Just the little things: "Sex is celebration, not apology. It was my time with my son, and you stole it. You double your mileage with your gifts to me by bragging about them. Vacations with your folks are more work than play. It's only a car, dear. Would you please rethink your role as wife? Your house, my bills. There was nothing wrong with what you did, except that I felt abandoned at our own party." All of these a clutter of pique and selfishness, a brief loss of caring, a raw irritability, and just plain spite. So much for guilt. I never once meant to hurt you, nor you me. We always knew that guilt trips were such a waste. Straight-arrow friendships are rare, and even then seldom real. We do not offer cheap grace. We have learned to forgive.

I love you!

Warren

The Need to Confront

Confrontation in friendship usually means that anger is aroused, either before, during, or after the confrontation. It is important that the anger be dealt with as creatively as possible. Dr. David Mace, dean of marriage therapists, has given us what I have referred to as his three R's of responsible anger. He urges that we first *recognize* the anger for what it is, call it by name, just as soon as it arises. Secondly, we must be willing to *renounce* our right to vent it in fury, because fighting is not appropriate to a loving relationship. Finally, we should *request* help from our friend in exploring and dealing with the hurt feelings that triggered the anger.

Whatever our feelings as to what a creative use of anger is in the friendship of marriage, or however impossible it may seem to "keep the peace," it must be agreed that anger is a healthy signal warning us of trouble in the relationship, while fighting is most often destructive and to be avoided. If the confrontation should come to rage and what can only be called a fight, it is important that these eruptions be flushed. When the life channels between friends get clogged with what can only be called the *waste* of rage, in order to protect the integrity of relationships, it must be expelled, else the creative channels are polluted and the poisons of anger suffuse the entire human exchange.

Blocking. It may be dangerous to your health and that of the relationship to refuse to pay attention to your anger, no matter how inappropriate the feeling may seem to you. My colleague, Tom Green, recently mystified a client, after the client's recitation of severe marriage problems previously undisclosed to anyone, when he asked if she also had problems with constipation. She admitted that she had been pestered by acute problems of that nature for years.

There are many reasons for blocking anger. In some homes the expression of anger is forbidden on religious grounds (anger is sinful), or because a parent cannot emotionally cope with the upset. In other homes, one parent rages about and terrifies the others: anger becomes the enemy. If parents quarrel endlessly, children may decide that disagreements lead to arguments and grinding noises and ugly words to violence: anger is frightening. When children escape these homes, they may have trouble managing anger creatively.

When Allen was growing up, only his father was allowed to get angry. Mother whispered around the house, warning the children, "Now don't upset your daddy. You know how he gets." Out of this came an adult son who imitated his father with a terrible rage, breaking furniture and clearing bars with his bare fists. The skinny, pale daughter was hurt and pouting most of the time and unable to discuss with her husband the things that angered her. Another son was a policeman who looked perfect, but was arrested for operating a huge, sophisticated burglary network.

Beth's parents had said, "Christians do not get angry." She and her sister were not allowed to yell at each other, much less scrap. Beth began to suffer migraine headaches at seventeen when sister, thirteen months younger and looking very mature, "stole" Beth's boyfriend by promising sex. Beth was enraged but felt she could do nothing; so she sat by and watched her sister come and go with her former boyfriend. As a wife, Beth was no better. The headaches persisted, and guilt blocked her expression of anger. When asked what she did with her anger, she said, "I pray." When asked about the headaches, she answered, "I take my medicine and go to bed, sometimes for two or three days." The headaches punished herself, and going to bed punished her husband, whom she saw as selfish and untrustworthy.

Mary was from a suppressed German Lutheran family in Iowa. No feelings of any consequence were expressed. She could not recall being touched by her father, and her only clear recollection of her mother touching her was when she brushed her hair. This was usually a painful experience and unhappily associated with mother's hands. Mary's husband described her as cold, mousey, quiet, and not interested in sex. Her face was set, and her eyes seemed clouded over. Nothing ever really excited her, and she felt that life was meant to be endured, like intercourse. Their pastor had sent them to me after Mary's husband had asked for a divorce.

To block anger is probably one of the most physically damaging things a person can do with feelings. Anger is an energy that must go somewhere. We ignore it at our peril, because just when we think we have successfully suppressed it, we find that our body is complaining with aches and pains, and perhaps severe illness, or we are taking the anger out on the wrong person.

We block by *denying* (It's not important); by *pretending* (He didn't really mean it); by *excusing* (I probably would have done the same thing if I were in his shoes); by *martyring* (It's my fault); and by *delaying* (I'll let it go *this* time). Behind these dams accumulate the enormous energy of anger, which may begin to contaminate the body systems of the person as well as the relational systems of the friendship. Under extreme circumstances, either or both may even in fact die from it.

Discharging. Once a decision is made to acknowledge and own the anger, it is possible then to decide how best to discharge it. Here again, talking and touching may be necessary. Ideally, we should be able to tell our friend that we are angry and cause a discussion to come about in which the anger is dissolved. The key here is for our friend to take us *seriously,* accepting the fact that we are really and truly angry, regardless of how he or she feels about the anger—that is, whether it is justified, appropriate, or properly targeted on him or her. It is best when the anger is honored, so to speak, as something that we have a *right* to have. Only then can a healthy discussion follow as to what can be best done about it. Talking through is often a painful and frightening process. Consequently, we are tempted to avoid it, which can be even more dangerous.

Occasionally, even the talking is not enough. A person may be heard and accepted, but the accumulation of anger is just too great and cannot be expelled through talking. With me present, I have encouraged couples to use a cushion to bang on the one who is the target, providing both agree to such an exercise. While both know it is a mock battle, they have been able to get anger out and transferred, and even symbolically to "get back at" the other, without engaging in some destructive behavior inappropriate to a successful resolution of the problem.

Dorothy said to Ted after he admitted to having an affair, "I'm furious with you. I could just shake you within an inch of your life. Why did you do such a thing to us?" No reason could be found except that the other woman was attractive and willing, and Ted was interested. Ted agreed to letting Dorothy pound on him with a cushion for a few moments. He covered his head and she banged away. Ted did not feel humiliated and did not rise angry when Dorothy finally threw the cushion at him and said, "Get up, you bum." He peeked out, and got up looking somewhat chagrined.

Dorothy, not a large woman, then slapped at him. He ducked, and she threw herself into his arms sobbing. After three or four minutes of crying, she stopped, blew her nose, and announced, "Okay, Stud, let's go home." In a few subsequent sessions we talked further about causes and results, and how such experiences might be avoided. The marriage has survived two years since their brief therapy and seemed healthy when I spoke to both of them recently at a workshop.

Resolution. Anger is your friend in that it has signaled that you are unhappy. To deny the presence of anger is as foolish as denying the presence of fever. Getting the anger out to someone—the implicated party or another friend or counselor—permits the discharge of the distracting and disturbing energy. It may allow for a resolution of the problem and the reaffirmation of the relationship. While the precipitating event may be so destructive that discharging anger is not sufficient to dissolve the event, the person is *emptied* of hostile, damaging feelings, and *both* parties know the intensity of the pain, hurt, and ruin of the experience. This knowledge can be critical in dealing with guilt feelings, as well as equipping both to avoid precipitating events of alienation and disaffection in the future.

If the event is not fatal for the relationship, a resolution should come. Out of the fight emerges new *understanding,* the asking and giving of *forgiveness,* with a promise and *contract* to guard against that sort of thing in the marriage, or at least to be more alert and handle it more effectively if there is a next time.

The sequence, then, is something like this:

1. Get in touch with your feelings as quickly as possible after any signal of being disturbed.
2. What is the feeling? Name it. If it is anger, acknowledge it to yourself. Claim it. Own it.
3. Locate the source of the anger: who, when, where, how, why, simply and clearly.
4. Address your friend, *privately* if possible, and from your *adult:* "When you did (said) that, I felt angry toward you. I want to discuss it with you."
5. Insist that your anger be honored for *discussion,* even if your

friend feels it is inappropriate.

6. Be fair. Hear his or her feedback. Search for an explanation that satisfies both parties, but do not explain *away* the feelings.
7. Get the feelings *out*. Talking should do it. If yelling is *necessary,* remember that this can greatly alarm children and further inflame your feelings. Do a *ritual pounding* with a cushion if both agree. Take care to protect sensitive body parts.
8. Ask and give forgiveness.
9. Contract to guard against recurrence.
10. Do something different. Take a walk or a bath together. Make love if you both want to.

The Need to Be Free

Friendships can become emotional traps. In marriage this is especially true. We begin to depend upon the safety and security of the relationship, especially if the trust level is good there and not so good everywhere else. Talking with the spouse is comfortable, easy, and familiar. Behavior requires fewer explanations, and innovation is often neither wanted nor expected. We can be lazy, sloppy, conventional, even hackneyed and banal, and the spouse will excuse us and simply hope for better. It is important, then, that we pay attention to our need to be free, so that we do not become victims of an overindulging spouse, or our own resignation.

Free to Discover Self. We lay a lot of heavy expectations upon the married relationship. Some marriages suffer because people try to get almost all of life done there. With little privacy and much intimacy, all of the play, entertainment, work, and community are attempted within the context of marriage and its immediate environs. Such a marriage can become ingrown and dull. Even those who genuinely prefer it this way miss out on the feeding and challenge of people and experiences beyond the marriage. The mirror idea is important in marriage and family. We become mirrors for one another as we live in each other's presence; and with the verbal and nonverbal reflections (feedback) which we receive, we are able to see how we are doing as persons and family members. To have a friend in marriage over a period of years who is an accurate and reliable mirror is one of the greatest gifts of marriage. Still, others can assist in this feedback.

Also, others may be more apt than the spouse to encourage us to move from mirrors to windows where we can look out to the moving, changing world that invites us to expand and grow.

Marriage should not inhibit the creative processes of the maturing adult to the degree that the person is diminished and unrealized. There are contractual limits that enable the marriage to thrive in trust, and the individuals to enrich their lives, but limits must not make marriage a prison which generates resentment and bitterness.

Marriage must provide for *privacy,* which we shall discuss more fully in chapter 4. Privacy means that I must allow time and space for me, to include not only grooming but also those things that permit me to feel that I am an entity without appendages of other people, and responsibilities. I need to feel that I have time and energy to *take care of me:* body, mind, and spirit. I may need time to read, think, reflect, write, paint, plant, or make something which says that *I am important; I respect my needs; I love me.* For it is only as I pay attention to my privacy that I am fit and able to move into relationship. A mother should not have to lock herself in her own bathroom just to have a little privacy and then have to be satisfied with the quality and quantity of *that.*

Jan had four young children. Her husband, Ev, was a linesman with the power company. There was not a lot of money, but there were no major problems regarding finances. Ev liked football and a little beer. He did not like housework or taking care of kids. When Jan collapsed from "nervous exhaustion," her physician referred them both to me. The major task was to help Jan make room for herself and get support for that program from Ev. We managed to get part of one day and one evening, which were hers to plan and use as she chose, with an allowance from the budget (Ev had one also) for "mad money." It made an enormous difference in her spirit and energy, as well as her attitude toward Ev and the children. The therapist toward whom he had been so hostile suddenly became his friend. "She's a different woman," he said. "Everybody's feeling better, even the baby." And it wasn't just a matter of giving Ev's servant a little time off. He became a supportive friend in the new patterns, getting supper, bathing children, and baby-sitting on her night off, as well as paying more attention to ways of helping at home, and relieving her of all of the directing, managing, and disciplining processes of the family. On her half-days she shopped, visited, or bowled with a friend. Some nights she just went over to her aunt's house, had soup and a sandwich with her, watched TV, and played one game of Chinese checkers. Jan laughed when she told me, and she said, "I know you think that's dumb, but I actually had fun." Ev played poker one night a week and got into some difficulty with his buddies when their wives found out about "Jan's *freedom.*"

A marriage should be strong enough to permit people to move out of each other's circle of expectations occasionally without the other feeling rejected or abandoned. A person should feel free to say, "We always watch this program, but I will read for a while and go to bed early tonight." Even promises to visit friends or relatives or to take in a movie should be *open to recontracting* when you need to do something for yourself which has a kind of urgency about it. The freedom to be alone within the demands for intimacy must be assured if autonomy is to be preserved and the person is to be nurtured.

Free to Cultivate Primary Relationships. Marriage is an *exclusive* relationship. There is no other experience like it. We have expectations, make commitments, and satisfy needs uniquely in marriage. The law permits only one husband or wife at a time. If a man and a woman are husband and wife, each is unique to the other, and the legal bond is exclusive.

From that legality flows any number of commitments that are exclusive to the marriage: the absolute exclusivity of their child's parentage; joint ownership of property; certain traditional public behavior, such as living together; private understandings; and the intimate promises of husband and wife. A marriage will hardly simultaneously tolerate another look-alike. Monogamy has not fared well in our so-called free society, even though women are more and more liberated. Certainly polygamy would not survive in a society of liberated women. Some argue for multiple mates for both husband and wife in marriage. The human being is remarkably adaptable. However, I am better convinced that a man and a woman entering self-consciously into an exclusive relationship and creating their marriage out of the incredible uniqueness of themselves can experience something extraordinary: the immense possibility of each Self, and each-in-union in the circles of intimacy. Marriage should also support each person's friendships among members of the *same sex*. Men and women relate in their same-sex, primary relationships in ways that are critical to emotional health. Something gets done there that seldom happens in any other relationships with mate, family, children, parents, or friends of the opposite sex. Topic, vocabulary, and style can shift dramatically with a same-sex, close friend. Some women still call it *girl talk,* even though they are apt to get the heavy-lidded condescending smile from those who see such women as unliberated. Whatever we call it among males or females, we need to check out how we are doing among our own sex, exchange the *in* talk, swap "helpful hints," spoof the opposite sex, and in countless ways exorcize the demons that mates plant in us. The gang is a sanctuary, a haven, and a retreat for some. For others, it is a brief respite; for all of us, a place to affirm ourselves and enjoy.

George and his father bred and sold dogs. They spent much time going to dog shows, and discussing their own animals on the phone. Otherwise they saw each other only on family occasions. George was not dependent on his father, and his father was not controlling. Lucile, George's wife, was jealous, saying it was unnatural for a grown son to spend so much time with his father. George was angry and hurt. He liked his father and was glad they were friends. Lucile was not interested in dogs, turning up her nose at "those stinking animals." For five years the dog question created a crisis in the marriage that took almost six months to resolve. Lucile never learned to share George's hobby, but she did come to respect the relationship he had with his father when she better understood how angry she was toward her own father who had rather cruelly rejected her.

Healthy marriages can permit primary relationships with members of the *opposite sex*. Many couples will feel this is the most dangerous freedom of all. We may avoid it in deference to the mate's uneasiness, or because we, ourselves, fear losing control of our emotions. *What if* . . . hovers about the most innocent relationship with a member of the opposite sex. *Be careful.* . . . guards interesting relationships of emerging closeness. *Hide it* . . . may shadow relationships that are clearly exciting, which signals *hide it* from the other person, yourself, or your mate.

One would think it unnecessary, but my work with married couples seems to require that we say here that a healthy marriage might allow for simple exchanges of affection, deep conversation, and innocent meetings between men and women who are not married to each other. The complaints I hear are from people who resent the mate greeting a person of the opposite sex with a hug or kiss, having a long, serious conversation with him or her at a party, or going to lunch with that person. I have yet to find a single instance of such behavior that was not safe, if not totally innocent. Most people who are going to "play around" are usually careful *not* to hug, kiss, touch, talk, or go to lunch so openly. I assume there are those who try to cover an affair with this byplay as a smoke screen, but most of us are not clever enough to hide the innuendo and subtle signals. Better to play it cool and keep the friendship that way. People who need an affair do not have to play the touching games. Those who touch and talk as expressions of genuine affection outside the marriage are sincere about those communications and would defend them even to an irate mate.

Two problems are usually posed. One is the domino theory which says that it is better not to get too friendly. This is like the teetotaler who says that a person would never become an alcoholic if one did not take that first drink. That is not an accurate cause-and-effect description of what creates an alcoholic. Nor does a hug, kiss of greeting, long talk, or lunch mean that we have the beginnings of an affair. We might, but the affair would not happen unless a lot of other things were going on in both lives and in the marriage that contributed to such an alliance. If a marriage is not strong enough to risk these simple communications of friendship, it needs attention.

The second problem has to do with people having to give up friends of the opposite sex just because they get married. The arguments are: most of those were romantic relationships (which is usually not true of *most* of them) and are better off retired from action; or the person should become the friend of both the husband and wife, which is often difficult to manage; or, the anxious mate will say, "I'm prepared to give up my old friends for you. Why can't you do the same for me?"

For this person that usually means that friends are easily discarded, or there is great anxiety about the possibility of extramarital relationships.

Actually, the primary, legitimate complaint from a mate in this matter usually has to do with one of them feeling embarrassed and neglected while the other gives attention to the friend. However, there are many marriages in which the couple know and experience each other's love, even as both maintain warm relationships with friends of the opposite sex. I think this can be an important sign of a healthy, adult marriage.

PARTNERS: MARRIAGE AS COVENANT AND CONTRACT

Along with its religious and cultural sentiments, marriage may also be seen as a small corporation, a business union of partners who have contracted to get needs met. Such a view in no way diminishes the social, aesthetic, religious, and personal values of marriage. Rather, it may help focus on the bonds and business of the relationship.

Let us consider two basic concepts: *covenant* and *contract*. Covenant is at the heart of the Hebrew-Christian tradition and dominates its literature. The oldest body of Hebrew law is called *The Book of the Covenant*. God had a personal covenant with Abraham, and later, through Moses, with Israel in *The Sinaitic Covenant*. Israel was to obey God's law in exchange for his grace. It was a comprehensive, life-embracing plan that suggests the intimacy of lovers: husband and wife, as in the book of Hosea.

Covenant ideas are also present in Christianity. Jesus is seen as *being* the new covenant promise of God. Jesus appeared as the love covenant, fulfilling the law covenant, that was binding upon his followers. There is the metaphor of Jesus as Bridegroom and his church as Bride.

Hence, the concept of covenant is woven into the fabric of our culture. It carries in it deep implications for integrity and commitment. Rising out of the heart of our two major religious faiths, covenant is the ultimate bonding of lovers. It is a signal to the world of interdependency welded in alliance.

Marriage as *covenant* is a relationship in which husband and wife commit themselves to each other in a *quid pro quo* arrangement, promising faithfully to respond to each other's needs and gifts. The covenant says: *I want to do life with you.* It is a broad and deep commitment, a bond of pairing and joining. So long as both are sworn, the trust is inviolable.

The *contract* is different. It is less permanent, a rule of the game, which can be renegotiated at any time and simply tells us how it is between us just now. The covenant says: *I want to do life with you.* The contract says: *And here is how, now.*

It is important to use these two words to differentiate between the promise and bond as contrasted with rules and arrangements. Couples would not be so alarmed if they would use covenant and contract differently. Only the death of the relationship dissolves the covenant. Mutual agreement renegotiates contracts, which are the working tools of the marriage. Marriage is covenant. The *business* of marriage is done by the ever-changing contracts, which may be simple understandings or hard-fought agreements, arrived at after deep searching and hard work on both sides. It is easy to see that it is in the partnership idea of marriage that the ability to negotiate needs becomes critical. The skills of dialogue, the management of feelings, proper perceptions of reality, a gift for compromise, and the ability to keep one's word are the tools of negotiation. Contracting in marriage is an art that must be continually practiced and refined.

Eva and Ralph came for counseling after five years of marriage, when it became clear that Eva, at twenty-eight, required a complete hysterectomy. Ralph was depressed, suppressing anger and disappointment. Eva was the youngest of three girls, and her oldest sister had been adopted. She was sad about her loss, but felt they could adopt children. Ralph was an only child of successful parents, who had considerable ego investment in their son, an attorney as was his father. His parents had never approved of Eva and used the news of her hysterectomy to ask some disturbing questions. His mother even said, "I would think, Ralph, that it would be impossible for you to love someone who could not honor your manhood with a child."

In the first session Ralph was quiet. Eva talked, weeping softly now and then, as Ralph cautiously patted her hand. When asked what he was feeling, he said, "Sad, sad for her. It's a great disappointment, you know. She really wanted children." To a further question he said, "Oh, sure. I had my heart set on fathering my own child." They had spoken briefly about adoption, and he was clearly suffering from the loss of a chance to *father* a child.

Later I spoke alone with Ralph. He was not happy about the thought or prospects of adoption. Babies were not plentiful. But there was something more. "Maybe I want out of this marriage. She is half a woman. I am a whole man. I don't want to raise just any child. I want to see *my* wife carrying *my* child, from *my* sperm. Is that too much for a man to ask? Hell, if I had known this would happen, I doubt I would have married her." He was angry, his voice in a strong stage whisper. I waited. He was pensive. His eyes filled. Then he looked at me and said, "How the hell do you tell a woman *that*? Only an S.O.B. would leave her now."

The covenant had been: I want to do marriage with you. The understood contract had been: And there shall be children. The contract could not be honored and would require negotiation. The covenant was threatened, but it was not automatically up for grabs. Ralph still seemed to want his marriage. We went on from there.

Eva was afraid Ralph would leave her. "He adores kids, and there is such family pride, especially on his father's side, what with Ralph's three uncles and all their kids. Ralph is an only child, and his folks always want the best from him. Now look."

"At what?" I asked.

"At me. I've ruined everything. If I were half a woman . . ." she paused, shocked at her own pun. "If I had any guts, I'd offer him a divorce."

"But what about adoption?" I asked.

"I'm afraid to talk about it any more. He does not want just any kids. He wants *his*. Besides, I really think his folks would reject an adopted child." She felt helpless.

In all our sessions both Ralph and Eva expressed anger and fear as we tried to sort out the contract options, never accepting the idea that the covenant was in jeopardy.

Further sessions enabled us to examine all the gifts and promises of their covenant. Ralph became more autonomous regarding his parents and more supportive toward Eva. They found ways to enhance the marriage and spent more time doing the things they enjoyed early in their relationship. They quit agonizing over the child question. They confronted his parents with their rejection of Eva. They reaffirmed their marriage to his parents, who visibly warmed toward Eva. The marriage deepened and expanded. Eva began night courses toward her master's degree in elementary education. They entertained more, played more, took long weekends out of town, and moved to a condominium on a lake where they could sail. With their friendship nurtured, their love life became "fun, even *funny* sometimes," as Eva described it, "and for the first time, not so serious as before."

Then, after about six months of weekly sessions, Eva called me early one morning to say that Ralph had asked that they talk again about initiating adoption procedures, and for that he wanted them to take a long weekend in Boulder. As she canceled the appointment for Saturday, she said quietly, "I feel so loved." It was working out. Six years later the marriage was alive and well, with Mark and Daphne added to the family.

A part of the process in this marriage crisis was to strengthen the *covenant* (I want to do life with you) when the *contract* regarding children threatened to destroy the marriage. The love and friendship were enhanced, so that the contract could be renegotiated. Once it was again clearly established that they wanted to do life together, the petty ego quarrels were seen for what they were, and ignored the second time around. Love was needing children, rather than the ego needing affirmation. Children in that family could then experience the most important factor in their own emotional health: *Parents who love each other.*

Partners do the business of marriage. There is a legal document called a marriage license. They jointly hold property, enter into contracts with utilities and business firms, earn and administer sums of money, parent children, and often become owners of business enterprises.

If we are to understand something of the contractual aspects of the business of marriage, we must examine the process of partnership.

Contracting in marriage is a daily business: Who will pick up the children? How shall we spend the evening? When shall we plan the vacation? Who will get snow tires for the car? The items change; the dynamics shift; but there are a few basic concepts that remain fairly constant in the process of doing partnership, and in that process some basic needs must get met.

Equality

In a marriage of autonomous adults, it is important for partners to feel like peers, equals, sharing mutually in the rewards or losses of the partnership. This has to do with respect. A man, having an affair with a woman while he was still married, said after some reflection, "Even if I get a divorce, I wouldn't marry *her*. I don't respect her. She isn't my equal. Does that mean I'm a snob?"

He was not a sexist nor a classist. She was *not* his peer, not in education, intelligence, interests, or values. It had nothing to do with snobbery. It was an honest recognition of critical differences. They were lovers of sorts but could not be partners. They would not have created an adult marriage.

In recent years we have heard a lot about equality. In the past there has been a trade-off of security for sex between men and women. Mutuality has begun to grow as women have discovered sex for themselves and learned to make money in jobs and professions that did not reduce them to role, function, or sex. There are many forms of prostitution. There is the old saw: "Every woman has her price, and for some it's marriage." Some women have felt prostituted in marriage. Sex was not for pleasure, but the product by which they bought for themselves financial security and respectability. When a woman works and earns a wage, she feels more like an equal with the man as they negotiate relationships. Even if women quit work to stay home at marriage or at the birth of the first child, there is still a new confidence and feeling of personal security. For years, I have had women report that they could not leave a bad marriage because they could not manage financially without the husband. Those who were determined managed to get out any way. However, it was true that to get a divorce would often have done violence to the life-style and opportunities of the family, much of which was critical to the health and welfare of the children. In theory it is easy to say, "An unhealthy marriage also does violence to a family." The notion of "Something is better than nothing" conditions the will, and a woman who feels helpless to earn her way will often stay put. It is, therefore, mandatory that feelings of equality be mutually shared by men and women.

This is also true of sex. As women have more recently become better able to appreciate their sexuality and their right to pleasure, they have been less willing to "trade it off" for security in a bad marriage. They are less willing merely to "permit and endure" intercourse when they no longer care for the man.

Since money is the ticket to almost anywhere in our society, and the man traditionally earns the family income, he has assumed a certain power and prestige which enhance his feelings of superiority and the woman's of inferiority (of being *spayed* as the female counterpart to *castration* by poverty) simply by virtue of his earning power. He often adds insult to injury by radically controlling *his* money or by refusing to allow the wife to work and earn *her* money. He resorts to the tired clichés of what his mother did, or the jungle nature of the business world, the lecherous character of other men, his own exhaustion and need of his wife as nurse, while at the same time implying that "woman's work" is easy and her freedom permits leisure, sunbaths, TV soap operas, and a generally casual life. Most women are enraged by these insults.

Mutual respect in partnership is not rooted in role, function, or sex. It is not determined by societal assignments for husband and wife, or notions about man's work and woman's work, or the stereotypes of "men are that way," or "that's just like a woman." It has to do with the ability to have a unique appreciation for the partner as a person with his or her personal gifts and needs. When our partner sees us uniquely, we feel esteemed and respected. It is this balanced, mutual respect that enables equality in the marriage. If I see my partner as inferior, I will not treat her as an equal. I will not adequately respect her. While unequals may be partners in certain enterprises, a healthy marriage demands equality.

Our best research today indicates that perhaps more than ever before young people are tending to marry *peers*. Now, if we can enable them to escape the stereotypes of role, function, and sex which tend to support notions of inequality, perhaps men and women can begin to treat each other fairly and reciprocally. There are some marvelous differences between men and women, but there is nothing that dictates feelings of inequality of persons, so that either is exploited or abused.

Commitment

In the business of marriage, it is the task of partnership to insure commitment. A friend may excuse himself. A lover is subject to moods. A partner is in the harness with you, pledged and present. It is pedantry to push the solo qualities of friend, partner, and lover. While distinct, they finally merge. However, I occasionally see a marriage saved—one that deserved saving—because one mate was genuinely committed to the alliance of partnership.

A man had a superficial friendship with his wife and was in fact committed to his work. He had trouble finding love feelings for her and seriously considered divorce. Only his pledge at the time of the wedding made him try. Then his wife had a serious auto accident. During her recovery he came to love and enjoy her again. Years later, just after his funeral, his wife said, "He wanted to leave me when the children were young. He stayed because of his promise. After my accident, we seemed to fall in love again, and our marriage lasted forty-two years." There may be many "if's" and "maybe's" in this woman's love story, but when I consider what might have been lost without the pledge or partnership, I know there is value in a healthy concept of unconditional commitment: "Come hell or high water, we are partners. What happens to you, happens to me."

If love turns to hate and friends become enemies, "partner" is meaningless and destructive, but often it is the *one* aspect that keeps people trying when it is hard to be friend or lover. It is more healthy for adults to work on the marriage because of their solemn pledge of partnership than, for example, to "stay in it because of the children." That puts the burden on the children, who have so much to gain by a good marriage between their parents, and so much to lose by a bad one. Unhappy mates then often turn to the children to justify staying in the marriage. They turn to them for love, achievement, obedience, and approval, with those parents often in open competition for their children's affection. How much better for adults to explore the strength of their word *not to quit* in the face of weak friendship and pale love.

It is in the idea of partner that we cement the relationship against the whims and vagaries of friends and lovers. It is here that the agreement between adults is finally tested for sheer determination, grit, and stamina.

If there is one general criticism that might be leveled against today's divorcing couples, it is that despite the increased effort of marriage counseling, *many couples give up too soon,* and after too little effort. Better grounding in the partnership aspect of marriage might help people hold on and work. Someone asked Winston Churchill why the English bulldog had such a flat nose, and he said, "So it can breathe without letting go." If there is some genuine commitment to being partners, a marriage may breathe without the couple letting go.

It is easy, here, to become emotionally trapped in a my-marriage-right-or-wrong loyalty to a relationship that has little to commend it. My plea is not for some sort of heroic fealty to a marriage that is little more than a piece of paper. Nor is the partnership concept only the knot at the end of the rope, or the arm-twister for *just in case.* The loyalty aspect of partner is rooted in the command function of oath: "You have my word that I will work on this marriage. Even if friend and lover are badly strained, I am still your partner, and between partners the word is *work."*

Negotiating Goals

Part of the work of partnership is negotiating compatibility between two autonomous adults. Strong people have strong opinions. Their feelings may run high. They call for action, and each may want to command. Their values may not always mesh.

The task is to put together a *third entity:* their *compromise.* This is a key word in partnership. Compromise means to promise *together.* Working partners, then, submit their own will to the harmonized wills of both and, in such a blend of the best of each, find the action model that may meet the needs of the partnership. A somewhat idealized analogy of the spirit of compromise between equals is the twenty-four chromosomes that each parent contributes in the conception of another human being. Each partner makes his or her limited gift to the creation of a *third entity,* a person who will not be exactly like either.

There are many ways to organize the process by which partners and families accomplish goals. Following are eleven aspects of this process, illustrated by what my partner, Dian, and I put together for our family when it became clear that I wanted a doctoral program.

1. Setting Goals

These often emerge out of everyday living. Personal needs, accidents, a challenge in the environment, even a revelatory moment as in a dream may cause one or both partners to focus on a goal that requires negotiation, special planning, and extra resources. Once, for us, a goal was focused when, on a New Year's Day, Dian and I each made two lists for the coming year: "What I want for me" and "What I want for you." Then we exchanged them and discussed the possibilities. Another time, a special anniversary challenged us to plan and save for a trip to England.

Some years ago after many conversations, it became clear to us that I should shift my career as a seminary professor to include counseling in a clinical practice. We also thought our family might profit from the inner-city experience of a great metropolitan center. Our life-style and financial needs with three children moving toward college also made it imperative that both of us complete our graduate degrees. We had always talked together in the late evening, and those times began to be consumed by these three goals.

2. Establishing Priorities

Goals pile up. Some are more important than others. Some are clearly feasible, others only marginally. Some are short-term, while others will take time. Some are foundation, and others are superstructure; they build on each other.

I needed and wanted a doctorate. Dian needed her master's degree if she were to command the position that could carry a major part of the family budget during my graduate program. Stephen, age sixteen, was near completion of high school. It might be possible for both him and me to enter schools in the same area, and he could live with us in order to reduce expenses. Jennifer, thirteen, and David, eleven, were excited about the move.

3. Developing Alternatives

One of the greatest causes for pain in the partnership is a win/lose mentality. What is needed is a *win/alternative* process, so that if the top priority is impossible, the partnership does not give up in despair. If you feel like a loser, it may be because you are setting yourself up with a formidable goal that has little chance of success, with the only alternative being loss and defeat.

Our first choice was the professional doctorate program at Chicago Theological Seminary, with my study including clinical work and a research fellowship at the University of Chicago Hospitals. If this were denied, we would try elsewhere. Other schools were investigated. Even if I were accepted, there might be housing problems, or difficulty with Dian finding just the right teaching position. We considered, in that eventuality, my commuting once a month to our home in Kansas City. If Steve could not complete high school early, he would remain behind with friends. If he did graduate, we would try to get him in the Chicago Art Institute and the University of Chicago. If that failed, he would go to a state university in Kansas or Missouri.

4. Assigning Tasks

This phase usually has to do with gathering data, saving money, and investigating. It is what is referred to in business as a *feasibility study* and has primarily to do with preparation that will give clues as to the possibility of winning the goal.

I had to get myself accepted into the program. Dian would need to complete her M.A. Steve had to accelerate his high school program by adding courses and attending summer school. Housing for the family and a job for Dian had to be found. Everybody got busy.

5. Checking Risks

Important goals often involve heavy risks. These must be openly and honestly faced, so that adequate defenses may be organized for protection, and also in order that these might not be used as *excuses* to fail.

One risk for the family would be moving to Hyde Park in Chicago, an island in one of the world's most troubled ghettos. The impact of the culture shock upon the children was threatening. The financial security of the family was a concern. Then there was always the possibility of academic problems causing the program to be lengthened beyond the family's endurance. We knew the risks and discussed defenses against them. Our plans rolled on.

6. Making Decisions

Decisions were made through family conferences, letters, survey trips, phone calls, and interviews. The family was in accord on both our priorities and alternatives. Each one felt that his or her personal needs were being taken seriously and met. We mobilized our resources for a major educational experience for all of us.

When I was accepted for the program, the final decision to attend had to be made. It was decided that Dian would attempt to complete her M.A. during the summer while I began my work in Chicago. Steve agreed to forfeit his summer plans in order to attend summer school, as well as earn as much money as possible teaching art at a church in the ghetto. He would also apply for admission to the Art Institute of Chicago. A decision was made for the family to join me in Chicago in September. Dian would apply for teaching jobs in Chicago, and we would investigate housing once she found her school.

7. Taking Action

After all the planning and arranging, all the interviews, calls, letters, budgets, and loans; after all the careful blueprint and construction, there comes that magic moment when all systems are "go" and our "show is on the road." It is the moment of ignition—a last phone call, an airplane send-off, packing the moving truck, and the early morning exit—something that says, "Now!"

Our lift-off came with my leaving for Chicago in June with our tired, old station wagon, which we could easily risk parking on the streets of Chicago (we had fantasies of auto-cannibalism). Dian and Steve entered summer programs in Kansas City. Dian received her M.A. degree on the hot, sad day of Robert Kennedy's funeral. Steve finished high school a year early and was admitted to the Art Institute of Chicago. Dian was hired by Harvard-St. George, a private school in Chicago where Jenny and Dave would also attend. We found an apartment only a few blocks from the university and Harvard-St. George, in a community of other graduate students in my program. In August I returned to Kansas City to move the family to Chicago in a rented van. Our first drive down Lake Shore Drive into the city was beautiful. We were excited. We were days away from the Democratic National Convention. A mood of foreboding was building in Chicago. But life seemed good. Our plan was working. We were not apprehensive. Taking action felt good.

8. Carrying Through

Carrying through means not running out of gas, crashing, or having to declare financial or emotional bankruptcy. It means keeping the plan alive, responsive to the dynamics of daily change, and realistic adjustment to what will work toward the ultimate goal.

The Chicago sojourn was tough. There were many difficult times: struggles in the neighborhood, money concerns, academic stress, children under pressure, and the constant feeling of having to adapt to a sort of "camping out" life-style. We had family conferences, shared at least two meals a day, attended church on Sunday, and sought out the fascinating shops, museums, galleries, theaters, parks, dunes, and beaches in and around the Windy City. We ice-skated on the mall and swam at the pool of the university. We made new friends and did our share of the entertaining. Steve was robbed at knife point and lost a precious forty dollars earned at a tough job acting in a street theater cast in ghetto performances. I put together a book of poems called *Bruised Reeds,* and a new friend, David Breed, did the photographs. It was published the next spring. Steve liked the Institute, and Dian, Jenny, and Dave had a good year at Harvard-St. George. My doctoral program was exciting and demanding. There was good dialogue between my peer group and our professors, who were extraordinarily open to new ideas and processes in education and psychology, both of which seemed up for grabs in those days. My clinical work and research fellowship at the University of Chicago Hospitals were most challenging, and I especially appreciated taking a seminar with Elisabeth Kübler-Ross on death and dying. We were more than surviving; we were flourishing.

9. Doing Evaluation

Checkups occur along the way. Periodic inventories of "what's finished" and "what's left" are constantly falling away and rising in one's mind. Check lists, revised budgets, refrigerator notes, a new book, and special counsel for new input—all may contribute to the ongoing process of evaluation. At the end, when it is over, a more formal critique may be helpful, especially if the IRS is interested, or still further programs are to emerge out of this one.

The process may be totally *informal* with a simple, "Well, we won't try that again," or "Wasn't that a great experience!" This is the most neglected part of any venture, and it could be the most valuable for the future. I once counseled with a man who was fifty-three years old, had failed three times in his field, and had twice declared bankruptcy. A critique somewhere along the way might have been helpful.

However, for those of us who overdo analysis, critique, and evaluation, I would call to mind Viktor Frankl's injunction in his book, *The Unconscious God,* when he reminds us that the hunter's boomerang returns to him only when it has failed to hit the target. We turn back upon ourselves in prolonged reflection and diagnosis only when there is not something better to do that we do well. For this reason I felt it important to add number 11 to this process "Returning to Go." Evaluation is mandatory, but it must not become an end in itself. A man once said at a meeting, "It seems to me we spend most of our time revising by-laws. What *else* are we supposed to be doing?" Right action is the best message to the ego.

For us, evaluation occurred on many occasions, from our chats with one another "about things," to family conferences, to grades, report cards, and bank balances. A new look at calculation and calendaring occurred when we missed Dian's birthday. We knew the *date* but somehow had confused the *day,* which we had all projected as Thursday, and it should have been Wednesday. Birthdays are big at our house; so by ten o'clock on Wednesday evening when *nothing* like a celebration had happened, Dian was upset, to say the least. We celebrated the next day as planned, while signs also went up around the apartment reading, "Remember! *Next* year December 4 really does fall on Thursday."

Like so many other things in life and relationships, in any significant project we have to *keep checking it out.*

10. Celebration or Commiseration

The outcome of the program means either a party or a wake. It is important to pay attention to the grief process if a major goal is lost.

We hurt at those times. There is disappointment, perhaps even a deep sense of defeat and personal failure. There must be guards against depression and bitterness. Occasionally, it may even be helpful to talk it through with a trusted friend, counselor, or minister.

If the program is a success, everyone involved should find a way to celebrate. Tragically we tend not to celebrate our own little personal victories—promotions, completion of school projects, a new job, paying off a mortgage, or some other success. Birthdays or other important anniversaries deserve celebration and are excellent occasions for building a feeling of family or community.

There were parties in Chicago with other graduate students, their families, and later with old friends in Kansas City who had awaited our return. The program was a success in every way. We had even survived the truck-and-trailer exodus through the Chicago labyrinth when part of our caravan was lost and stranded. The family still celebrates as the children, older now, report things that continue to float to the surface and seem now alright to report to parents, some of which I am just as glad they sheltered me from at the time. The slides and home movies are celebrations, and we all keep asking for a showing on holidays.

11. Returning to Go

After it is all over, it is time to move on. A failure in the primary goal means commitment to the alternative. Success calls for moving to the next phase, and restructuring.

For us, it meant Dian finding a teaching position in Kansas City. I returned to the seminary faculty and immediately also entered private practice as a pastoral counselor, doing individual and couple therapy. Steve transferred his study program to another college. Jenny and Dave were glad to be back home with friends, even though all had changed a lot.

A new and exciting project faced us: moving from seminary faculty housing to our own home. Return to go!

Supporting Personal Life Goals

One of the most important tasks of the corporation is to help all members realize their personal life goals. More and more frequently in marriage counseling I find that young couples are conflicted over personal private goals. Yet there is a sense in which personal investment focuses differently in one's profession or avocation. A couple fought when the man decided he wanted to leave general medical practice and prepare for psychiatry. The wife did not see "why he *had* to do that" when it was so expensive in time and money after their years of sacrifice. A man was greatly annoyed with the upset to the household when his wife's knitting for fun turned into knitting for profit, as she began to take orders for garments, rent looms, and start her own shop. Personal goals may cause inconvenience and distress, leaving formidable blocks in the path of the partnership.

One way to approach discussion of life goals is to delineate four major divisions of the human experience: *privacy, intimacy, community,* and *transcendence.* These are obvious categories, and the infinite possibility of description defies neat definition. A target construct may help us to see how interrelated they are, how each grows from the other, and how transcendence embraces it all. A cylinder of layers would add a third dimension. A sphere would offer still greater possibilities of energy and motion.

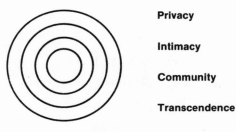

Privacy

Intimacy

Community

Transcendence

Privacy

One's private world is the sphere of unique need and aspiration. It includes aloneness but is a richer and more complex dimension than simple solitude or the sense of being alone even in the presence of others. Privacy is me in that inimitable drama of me experiencing *me experiencing.* Privacy has to do with paying attention to what is going on inside, of being aware of my total environment from the fall of light upon a field of wild flowers to a stomachache. Privacy is being by myself, letting things happen to me, or me directing my universe.

Taking one's self seriously is the first task of the autonomous adult.

This begins with the body, as the infant begins to notice hand or foot. One of the most important tasks of privacy is to make certain that body needs get met, so that the primary environment is secure, healthy, stimulated, and satisfied.

An overweight woman agreed that her biggest problem was that most of her pleasure needs were met with food. It was only when she took time to find pleasure elsewhere that she began to relinquish her compulsion to eat. Among these were guitar lessons, a cat, and a return to sewing for herself, which inspired her to lose weight. It is interesting to see how quickly people with weight problems lose the pounds immediately after a divorce, when they are seriously considering how others, especially the opposite sex, see them.

A young woman, who found herself busy with her career as a veterinarian, and the only custodian of her crippled mother, in an outburst of anger became aware of neglecting herself. She was able to focus attention on her own daily needs with the help of a deck of 3 X 5 cards. I asked her to write a simple treat for herself on each card, shuffle the pack, place them on her dresser, and turn one up each morning as gifts to herself. They were very inventive. Here are a few items on her list:

Take a short walk in the park.

Buy some fresh flowers or a new plant.

Listen to a favorite recording while doing nothing else.

Take at least a half hour for a bubble bath.

Start a new book that I have been waiting for time to read.

Get up early and greet the sun.

Do something neat for my body.

Start judo lessons.

Buy a new perfume.

Move in "slow motion" today.

Go to lunch alone at a different restaurant and think about some of the lovely moments of my childhood.

Write a poem for the first time since that creative writing course in college.

Give some special attention to personal grooming.

Start a savings account at the church credit union.

Work on my picture album.

Occasionally her schedule prohibited carrying out the instruction on the card; so she simply put it on the bottom of the stack, or somewhere along the way, and tried the next one. Once she said she had two cards turned up "to keep a special couple of things in sight," rather than losing them back to the deck. She did not feel guilty when she could not treat herself. After three weeks or so she caught the habit, gave up the card dictatorship, and simply permitted a place in her schedule for a spontaneity that celebrated her. The exercise engendered an awareness of herself as a person worthy of special privileges and the ritual of privacy. She learned to take pleasure *in* herself and *for* herself.

It is not fair to expect someone else to love us if we cannot "make love" to ourselves. It is important not to do only an imaginary trip, or simply to run errands for our daily support, such as buying vitamins or picking up the dry cleaning. We can give ourselves a treat that can mean as much as a present from a friend.

A single woman decided she had to learn to masturbate as a love gift to herself; she did this not out of desperation and loneliness, but in a new spirit of self-acceptance and a healthy appreciation of sensuality. At age thirty-two she was happily tearful as she recounted experiencing her first orgasm. She said, "It was as though I became a woman last night. Is that stilly? If so, I confess it with a lot of good feelings of achievement and contentment. I thought I felt like a woman the night I lost my virginity, but this beat that by a mile."

Privacy comes out of a self-conscious desire to "find oneself" and "experience oneself" for information and delight. It is most often not *public* and has deeply to do with seclusion, secrecy, and solitude.

To discover self is the great frontier and probably the most exciting adventure available to each of us. Yet many people are made anxious in solitude. Body awareness can be frightening. "I can hear my heart beating in my ears," someone will say. "I just get scared when I am alone." Suppressed anxieties may bubble to the top; respiration and heartbeat speed up, alarming the person even more, perhaps bringing on feelings of dizziness and panic. For some, "being alone" may trigger a mild hysteria.

It is clear that we want privacy, even that we are clear about privacy as a human need. It has been observed that we Americans will not give up our automobiles until *all* gas runs out. It is also doubtful that carpools will ever become popular. We like that little private time in the car alone commuting or running an errand.

Enclosed in that little spaceship we feel unreachable by the world, so anxious for our response to its invitations, demands, and commercials. We are immune for a time, often bathed in stereo music of our choice on tape. In therapy sessions people report turning up the "radio noise" and screaming back at it or swearing at the announcers. "It's all irrational," one man said. "It does not even respond to what's coming over the air. I just scream out my noise against their noise. I yell about things that happened that day, or just because I feel that way." Privacy functions differently for each of us. Auto privacy for this man was his occasion for ventilating.

Over the years I have talked with many mothers who manage time for themselves late at night when the house is quiet, children and husband asleep, and the demands of the day met or safely at rest. They take time then for a glass of wine and the newspaper already old. One woman said, "It is then as though the little bits of me that I have left all over the house and neighborhood come home. I knit back together. It's like getting to a favorite theme in a Beethoven symphony. So busy, then so exquisitely serene."

A part of the business of partnership is to help one another get the need for privacy met. Within that sphere are certain special gifts to the mind, body, and spirit that can only be given to oneself if adequate time and space are set aside. It is a partner's *support* of our need for privacy that often makes it possible. If the partner makes us feel guilty for wanting privacy, or insultingly goes as far as one husband who asked, "What do you do in there all by yourself? That's the craziest thing I even heard of," we can expect either fury or hurt from the mate, with a resulting chasm widening between them.

Some of us need privacy in order to write, read, practice an instrument, work the ham radio, tinker with the car, paint, or take a walk. People can get awfully crabby over intrusions at those times. They may say, "You are interrupting my work, study, rehearsal," but what they really mean is that you are interrupting their privacy, an unconscious need to be alone.

We must support one another's life goals found only in the realm of privacy. The health of the person and the relationship may depend upon how well privacy gets done in the marriage. "Leave me alone" may sound like an outraged misanthrope, when it is actually the legitimate cry of a spirit besieged. We must learn to listen for requests for privacy from our partner and then support that retreat. It is both a gracious and a loving thing to give. To have your partner volunteer, "I'll take care of that. Why don't you take a little time for yourself?" is a beautiful gift to receive, and too often it is a surprise.

Practice privacy. Learn to be alone. Cultivate a gentle solitariness. Sponsor and encourage it in your partner. Privacy is a time for remembering and savoring, for meditation upon the substance and truths of our lives, a time to fantasize and contemplate the future. It is a time to let down, relax, to be nothing and just be—to worship, float, dream. It is a time to enjoy—a time for one on one, you on you.

Intimacy

Eric Berne structured human use of time like a target, moving from withdrawal as space beyond the target to rituals, games, pastimes, work, and finally, *intimacy* at the center or bullseye.

Yet, according to Claude Steiner in his book, *Scripts People Live,* Berne could not define intimacy, except as the absence of something else. He doubted that it is possible for anyone to attain intimacy, and, if it were, a person would be lucky to know fifteen minutes of intimacy in a whole lifetime. Why posit something so central to human relationships if it cannot be defined or experienced?

Intimacy, as I speak of it here, is reserved to describe a quality of relationship with another human being. I cannot be intimate with a pet rock. People have relationships of love and affection with birds and animals which they describe as intimate. I know these relationships exist, and I have no need for a semantic quarrel about the use of intimacy in this regard. Words are our servants. They change a bit sometimes in order to stay helpful. But I speak here of intimacy between people.

Intimacy is often the word used euphemistically for human sexual intercourse. Yet surely a couple could have intercourse and not be intimate. Further, if the substitution of "intimacy" for "intercourse" indicates something more than a mock modesty, we have assigned to mere coitus one of the noblest expressions defining depth in human meeting. Intimacy and coitus are not necessarily synonymous.

Still, I occasionally hear a woman report being forced by her parents to marry when the parents learned she had had intercourse. A forty-six-year-old woman said her father required that she marry the young man when he caught them "having sex."

"I wasn't even pregnant. Besides, I didn't want to marry Bob. He did, but I didn't. You wouldn't believe the guilt feelings my father put on us. When I look back now, it's really funny. Not funny-funny, but laughable."

It was as though her father believed that intercourse caused some irrevocable union between the man and the woman. When he caught them having intercourse, in his mind it was as though they had been fused in a mystical bond that was the most profound and holy experience given to human beings. Nothing could then separate them. She quoted her father as having said:

"Once that happens, there is no turning back. You belong to him and he belongs to you. That's as close as two people can get. Now you'd better start your wedding plans."

It is true that many people have the most intimate feelings *during* intercourse. They may feel *fully known,* as the word is used in Hebrew thinking on this subject, and they *know.* They feel *loving* and *loved.* Yet the two should not be confused. Intimacy has to do with the character of a relationship. Intercourse is coitus, a union of male and female genitals.

In the spirit of Alexander Lowen's theories of bioenergetics, especially as found in his book, *Pleasure,* I believe that intimacy is a need that is very much a part of the body and its receiving systems. Most of us need to have our bodies accepted, appreciated, enjoyed, and loved. One might say:

"I am in here, and it is impossible to separate me from my body.

When you touch my body joyously, you touch me in ways that seem to say, 'It is good to be so close to you.'"

Sometimes it is almost a necessity to be embraced. There is a hunger for a hug, the most affirming gesture of the human family. To be whispered over, touched, and kissed—the barriers against the world's encroachment fall—we are tenderly laid bare in our quest for love; and like a deep breath, it cannot be saved for later. Intimacy is an ongoing, daily need.

That is why our world is so full of lonely people. They are emotionally starved. What is intimacy? Once at a workshop I asked the group for definitions and someone said, *"Intimacy is privacy shared."* This is like an oyster shell: a good place to make a pearl. It is a beginning and enables us to use what we have already said about privacy. It reminds us that real intimacy depends upon the quality of our privacy.

If I have loved *me* well, if I can feed my own spirit and take into my own hands my own body and not be ashamed; *then* I may be able to reach out without a crippling fear of rejection, share my private world of me, and receive another's. It is then that we begin to close the distance that makes loneliness and close the doors for a while against the loneliness of being creatures who can reflect upon our condition: to be human is to be alone. Intimacy is like fire upon the wood: a better way to be consumed, in light and heat.

Intimacy is privacy shared. Relationships occur when we trust enough to participate deeply in one another's life. There is a sharing at the roots, and of rooted things: ideas, dreams, feelings, and activities, so that a kind of transplanting comes about, and we begin to appear in each other's lives. There may be only slight traces or dramatic metamorphoses, as we see the impact of one person's world upon another's.

The intimacy grows as *invitations* are given:

This is a copy of a book I very much have enjoyed and I want to share it with you.

A few of my very best friends will be there and I am dying for them to meet you.

I have never even thought of that sort of thing before. Give me a little time.

expectations rise:

I told Robin that's the way you would feel about it. I'm so glad you two talked.

I just would not have gone to the concert without you. Whom would I have talked with about it?

It's a cinch my folks will be crazy about you.

closeness develops:

I like me better when I am with you.

You don't have to say a word. I know what's going on.

Please hold me. This has been one of those days. I just need to be near you.

and *changes* occur:

It's a totally different experience with you.

The more we talk, the better I understand why you feel as you do.

I'm sorry. I was really wrong. Thanks for being patient with me.

Intimacy may occur within a variety of relationships. Friends and relatives may be present in a special way and share the deep concerns of our privacy so as to be intimately involved in our lives.

A father said he felt like praying only with his young daughter as she said her bedtime prayers. This usually followed a brief conversation in which they shared "the neatest thing that happened today," and "the worst." This was a time of intimacy.

Discovered by his wife in an affair, a military officer recalled that the best thing about the experience with his lover was that he could "talk and cry with *that* woman" when his daughter was on drugs, and he could not with his wife. "You don't know what that meant to me," he said. His wife had insisted that they not discuss it. "As far as I am concerned, she is dead," she had said. The deeper intimacy was in the talking and crying together.

A woman who sat for months at the bedside of her daughter, who was terminally ill with leukemia, said that when her husband sat across the bed from her, "I never felt so close to any human being in my whole life. He is a tender man."

Some people must find ways to break through great emotional barriers before they are free to engage in intimacy.

I once asked a young woman, whose husband had demanded a divorce two years after marriage, how she got loved. She did not know what to say; so I invited her to close her eyes and fantasize a scene in which she might experience a moment of true intimacy with another human being.. She sighed and relaxed. Immediately she looked troubled and tears came. When I asked her what was happening, she said, "I am about four years old. My daddy is home from Korea. I am beside his casket with my mother and grandfather. My grandfather is holding me up so I can see my daddy. *(Long pause)* For some reason I feel very happy. I feel good. He is dead, but I feel good. I am not crying. That is, not in the fantasy." When I asked her to open her eyes, she said, "I'm glad you asked me to do the fantasy. I was not allowed at the funeral. I feel closer to my father now than ever before." That fantasy marked her movement away from bitterness and seclusion and into genuine experiences of intimacy.

It is expected that most needs for both the grave and the glorious human exchanges will be met within the partnership. Hopefully, the kindly passions of the spirit, from a hallowed grief to the most erotic sexual experience, will occur in the partnership as each gives trustingly and receives the other with genuine welcome.

Community

My community constitutes the network of people with whom I share my world. This is a broad definition. More personally, my community is essentially family and friends, who are the social fabric into which my life is woven. It is among them that I feel free to talk, play, create, work, and relax in an atmosphere of acceptance.

The *family* is a commune, a community. One's supportive communion should begin there. Robert Frost said that home is the place where, when you go there, they have to take you in. But the family experience should be more than "have to" responses. A young woman said, "I was thirteen before I realized that no one in our family even said good morning. It seemed incredible that five people—all of them older than I—could have lived together so long without even a 'hello' in the morning. So, I just started doing it. My father responded right off, but my mother and two sisters were still grumps, and would reply with something like: 'What's your problem?' or 'Don't be late for school now!' or 'What's so good about it?' It was as though they were embarrassed or something."

The family is our first community. The basic ingredients of community are given or denied in that setting: security, acceptance, personal regard, trust, support, forgiveness, loyalty, and love. Words. But in these words are the nuclear elements of community. Without these elements the child flounders, and only by some miracle will an autonomous adult emerge.

The partner attempts to reestablish and maintain a new base of community in the family or marriage. There, each person is aware of the *centripetal* forces that pick up the members of the expanding community and put them in orbit around the core experiences of the primary relationships, beginning with the parents and extending through the family to the revivifying partnership.

The families of origin are drawn into the marriage. They meet cautiously, angrily, or cordially in a convergence of forces with a potential for community or chaos: note the differing examples of the Capulets and the Montagues of Shakespeare's *Romeo and Juliet* and the Webbs and the Gibbs of Thornton Wilder's *Our Town*. Partners move back and forth between the two camps, making a path and leading the way for those who are often strangers, or collapsing under the pressure of prejudice and resentment. Generally, it is important that both partners be acceptable to both families. When they are not, there is apt to be alienation and considerable pain, if not tragedy.

It is helpful if partners facilitate acceptance for each other. Occasionally, one partner may be called upon to stand up for the other, making it clear where his or her loyalty lies, and what attitudes will or will not be tolerated.

A man said, "It was disgusting to see my parents literally fawn over Melany after she converted, while her own parents loved both of us, even after she switched. You would have thought the world had come to an end when we married, and a year later my folks celebrated as though Melany had been raised from the dead. But, then we had our own private pleasure. Melany had actually *wanted* to make the change. It was genuine, and my folks thought it was for them."

Parents condition a marriage with signals of acceptance or rejection that can have enormous reverberations throughout the community. They can set up the couple for success or failure according to their attitudes, feelings, words, and behavior.

Partners are sensitive to each other's centrifugal, or expanding, network of relationships. This may include business associates, club members, clients, neighbors, and friends. It has to do with groups and institutions, as well as individuals who have deep personal meaning for the partner. It relates to bowling teams and church committees, painting classes and bridge clubs, tennis buddies and the book guild. In the multifarious expressions of the personality, each of us needs to identify what she or he is about in the community of persons who feed us and allow us to give to them out of our creative and celebrative depths. The community is our universe of public availability; we are like the artist who sets up an easel on the corner of a busy street where all can see the expression of the self in public, while at the same time going about one's task in a spirit of enormous, private satisfaction.

Partners participate in, encourage, create, and support community with and for one another. Couples in counseling report a variety of problems in this area:

The family is clearly not the top priority for the husband/father. The wife and children become resentful, creating either a wobbly unit with the shadow father haunting their spirit and activities, or a group of floating human islands, touching and talking in wistfulness and anger.

A partner is jealous of the other's friends and activities not shared in the marriage: friends at the office, a handball partner, bridge club, church functions, showdog owners, etc. Occasionally this has nothing to do with reasonableness, in that the other partner could "come along too," or that significant time is also invested in the partnership. It is simply a blind jealousy.

In a partnership of trust, such problems are more easily resolved if the quality of intimacy enables both partners to feel wanted and loved. Otherwise, it is hard to accuse someone of jealousy when that person feels neglected. Also, it is difficult to check out, since who is to say what is "enough" intimacy?

Jean addressed this subject with her busy husband and concluded, "All I'm asking is for just more of you. Not money. Not furs and jewels," she said with a plaintive smile. "Just more of you."

Dan's response was: "Okay. What do you want me to give up? Bowling? You want me to give up Tuesday night bowling? What am I going to tell the guys? 'Jean won't let me out on Tuesday night anymore? She says she wants *more* of me.' I can hear them laughing now—especially Hank and Tom." He was not smiling.

Such begging and protestations are usually symptoms of problems in the larger relationship—a game of "Hide-and-Seek," as we called it in chapter 2—in which one partner is always trying to find the other. In a stronger relationship, needs are announced, respected, negotiated, and satisfied, with breathing space left for each of them in their separate community activities.

In the expanding network of relationships, we both *discover* and *invent* ourselves. We are triggered, challenged, invited, and pushed into an infinite variety of experiences with all sorts and types of people. Each person in our community potentially offers us a different world. Entering that world, we not only encounter our friend, but we also are introduced to his or her *world,* peopled with others who share, in turn, bits of *their* world. They become fragmentary mirrors in which we get glimpses of ourselves moving through the space and time of our lives. It is in these exchanges that inventing and discovering occur and we grow. Communities are enriching and, in turn, the marriage is enriched. It may seem risky, but let each other go, and the returns are apt to be beautiful.

Transcendence

To transcend is *to go above, to overpass or exceed, to get beyond oneself.* In a general way, we are speaking here of an understanding of life that transcends the time and space limitations of privacy, intimacy, and community. We are concerned with questions dealing with the *meaning* of our existence. How do we attempt to "make sense" of life? What's it all about? Can we discover the purpose and ultimate goals for individuals and the whole human family? Does living finally matter beyond just staying alive and trying to enjoy it?

Religion, philosophy, and psychology have been quite self-consciously preoccupied with this "search for meaning." In the "Logotherapy" of psychiatrist Victor Frankl, this search is central to both his system and the therapeutic process. His book, *Man's Search for Meaning,* was written out of his soul-crushing experience in Nazi prison camps. Miraculously, he survived when many others did not. His survival might be at least partly attributed to his belief that life is intrinsically meaningful; that is, simply to live is meaningful, but our living is enhanced by our search and discovery of the more personal and explicit meaning of our individual lives. Frankl believes that every person is engaged in this search. He suggests that we may discover the meaning of life in at least one of three ways: (1) through some important accomplishment; (2) through experiencing some value in nature or the culture, such as work or love; and (3) through suffering.

Abraham H. Maslow, especially in his books, *Toward a Psychology of Being,* and *Religions, Values and Peak Experiences,* has focused much of his thinking and research on what he calls the "peak experience," a transcending moment when a person is deeply moved in what may be an ecstatic experience that often leaves the person significantly changed in both attitude and action. These may be revelatory events in which we are shown something of the deeper meaning of our lives. We may, in them, be given direction or instruction concerning how better to explore and experience that meaning. It is assumed that the mystical experiences in the lives of the saints and spiritual leaders of history were absolutely critical to their revelations and reached to the core of their messages.

Frankl is centrally occupied with the "search for meaning." Maslow focuses on what he calls his concept of "self-actualization," which has to do with our becoming fully realized as persons. For me to explore my experience as a thinking, feeling, acting, and believing human being is a search for meaning. The meaning of *me* is clarified and given unity when these come together harmoniously. These aspects of me—when integrated and made congruent—constitute the *me* that I am about. However, the poets and saints have insisted through the centuries that life is somehow more, and that more may be suggested in Maslow's "peak experience." These bold moments of spiritual drama and revelation which confirm or open *the way* for us seem to come when we are struggling to bring unity of thinking, feeling, acting, and valuing to a point of belief and commitment. It is then in this belief and commitment that we make promises, take risks, invest ourselves, and move out upon the way of growth, enrichment, and self-actualization.

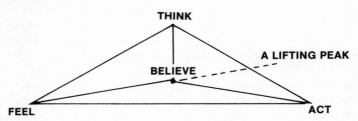

The peak experience becomes a transcending (mountain peak) event in which my integrating self rises above what is considered my "daily routine" and lifts me in a gripping movement of serenity and insight. Life becomes *four* dimensional.

The story of Christ's temptation on the mountain at the outset of his ministry and the legend of Gautama Buddha receiving enlightenment under the Bo tree are two of the more familiar examples of this harmonizing, focusing, and committing process in the lives of great religious leaders. Similar events of meaning and enlightenment occur every day among men and women who take seriously their own pilgrimage, and who want to come to an understanding of themselves in the universe. Some seem to *peak,* and *mean,* and *actualize* in a *Yea-saying* stance in which they say *Yes!* to life with affirmation and celebration. Others seem to be *Nay-sayers*: life is realized in denial of things, or of fortune, or even of reality. What we think life is, it is not. Just when we think we have discovered meaning, life is most meaningless. The search goes on. Some believe that the meaning of life is that life is nothing. H. L. Mencken is reported to have said that mankind is a fly on the wheel of the dung cart of the world. If that is true, we are of all creation the most miserable and deprived, and perhaps we deserve to perish.

The meaning question can sound abstract and removed from life. But if Frankl is correct in assuming that the search for meaning is what all of us are about, then the search is at the very *center* of life. The search goes on in the building of empires, in the monumental works of art, in great pioneering enterprises, as well as in the more modest activities of earning a living, growing hybrid roses, building a jogging record, changing jobs, studying star maps, abandoning old habits in search for a new experience, watching a tiny baby awaken, wondering about dandelions, avoiding the dentist, and just about everything else we do. All of life seems to fall broadly somewhere along the thrust-line of our lives, a line called "search for meaning." This transcending quality of life stretches all the way from a dogwood blossom to Thornton Wilder's "Mind of God."

Even though the search goes on for each of us, we must find ways to *declare* meaning: my life means *this* at center, *now.* In a support group I once asked for members to write their own obituaries in which they might suggest something of the meaning of their own life experience. Here are a few of the responses:

I have tried to become a first-rate educator.

I spent most of my life trying to discover the real meaning of intimacy with a woman.

I only wanted to enjoy it all in a healthy way.

I have worked hard at keeping life simple and honest, and it felt good doing that.

I suppose I just tried to "get it on" with God.

I have pursued music like an ardent lover. It searches my soul like a comet lighting the heavens.

Meaning? If there is any, I've missed it; but then it seems that I have missed out on just about everything anyway. Who knows what anything means?

To say that the search for meaning is in everything we do is, perhaps, to say that it is in nothing. Therefore, the process involved in the will-to-meaning has more to do with *how we handle the material of our lives*. For instance, a man said, "I have a hard time appreciating 'good' music. Oh, I like it okay, I guess. But I prefer 'blue-grass.' But this city needs an orchestra. I support that. I give a good bit of money to it. Maybe if I do, it will encourage others to do the same." It is a worthy thing to be about. He is helping to create an environment for the appreciation of all music, including "blue-grass." Someone else might not go about it this way. He does, and it adds meaning to his world.

Partners are in the business of marriage in order to further the welfare of both their separate and combined enterprises. To be alert to each other's changing needs and goals is a primary task of partnership, for it is in this intimate dialogue that support, encouragement, and fulfillment are most sure to come. It should be clear that unless there is the covenant/contract commitment to the hard work of doing life together, the possibility of either abandoning the other for a "new friend" or a "better lover" is considerably increased. It is in this sense of the marriage as a duly constituted, legal, working organism with realizable goals shared with a co-partner that a man and woman are most apt to feel the security and substance of their experience together.

LOVERS SHOULD 5
FEEL LOVED

A common expectation of marriage is that in it one has a guarantee of love. Friend and Partner is under promise also to be Lover. Of all the people in the world *this one* has pledged "to love and to cherish," no matter what words were used—traditional or contemporary. Words, symbols, and witnesses converge in a marrying way to give a seal of commitment, the assurance of a nurturing affection beyond any required elsewhere or expected from any other. "This one truly loves me!"

To some, these expectations are arbitrary and contrived, fatuous and like a sugar castle of improper demands, and absurd hopes. I once heard John Updike say that we " put too much on a marriage," expect more than any relationship can give. Nevertheless, we all try to slip past the rhetoric and poetry of the ceremonial love trysts and search the vast niagara of messages from Lover for the clear assurance of unconditional acceptance and grace. More than all else, *this* one, *here, now*—love!

It is from this Lover that the best of love is expected. It is in this celebration of the mating of us-persons that we hope to give love at a depth and with an extravagance that shall be for us a sign of arrival in a relationship of trustworthy and predictable devotion. Some believe that such mutually given promises will bring a new *wholeness* ("All I need is your love, and nothing can stop me."); *moral perfection* ("Love is the Great Commandment. Our love makes it possible for me to love all those other folks."); *body health* ("Our love invigorates me. The depression is gone."); *peace of mind* ("Life was hell until you told me you loved me, and suddenly I have enormous peace, a feeling that everything is going to be okay."). In the years of my practice I have heard all of these and more from the very young in premarital checkups to middle-aged divorcees on a high adventure with new love. These paeans to the miraculous powers of love reflect our deep need to know that here is love in endless supply, an alchemist's dream of translating "base" to "precious," "like" to "love," "I" to "we," "now" to "forever."

Yet, love at the Gate of All Things Possible is more than a magic show. It is a birthing of something small and splendid, too fragile to go unattended, and too full of the promise of its parentage to be taken for granted. It is in this *promise* that hope resides: "I promise you, and hope to be able to keep those promises."

The love story begins to be written. If like most, it may be flawed and raveled, littered with broken promises and quickly mended dreams. Friendship keeps lovers talking and touching. Partnership helps them work at the contract, so that in the loving they may get hope done, make it real. But as Lovers they enter a mystery: the beckoning, analogue cloud-figures (It looks like) by day and the fire-spirit (We are one) by night that draws lovers on, not to some Promised Land in which all promises are realized, but to the next gift of love between them when life is made good, again and again. Those who love this way know its truth and ultimacy. They are the ones who are able to spoof their own love. And they are also the ones who are most apt to have enough to spare, and the ones most apt to share it.

In promise and hope is the making of love, not *out of nothing (ex nihilo),* as in Hebrew thought, so much as *out of the available,* as in Greek thought. Our word "poet" comes from a Greek word which means to make or to fashion. How then do we make love happen for us?

"And how, my dear, do you know he loves you?"

This

"He says so.
He acts like it.
He wants to marry me.
He is all I ever wanted.
He made love to me."

Or

"My heart knows.
We act like lovers.
I feel loved.
I believe him."

Who knows? Either can be deceived. We look for a lodestone, a talisman, a formula—something that takes the guessing out of "How can we be sure?" *Making* love is no conjured thing, but something done in the time and space elements given to a man and woman for talking and touching. *Making* love is the keeping of old promises and making new ones. *Making* love is the fashioning of oneself in the presence of another so that both are loved, and feel that way.

Care

We begin with caring. Love is made in caring. To care for someone is to *pay attention* to that person. I am mind-full. I am careful not to be forgetful, else she may say, "Sometimes I feel you just do not care about me." I notice her, may call attention to her in ways that make her feel cared *about*.

A wife complained to her husband that she felt uncared *about* when he talked with his parents by long distance. "I have timed you and your folks talking for as long as thirty-five minutes without you so much as mentioning me once." It did his cause no good when he thoughtlessly said that his parents had not asked about her.

One of the great speeches in Arthur Miller's play, *The Death of a Salesman,* occurs when Willie Loman's wife defends him to their ridiculing sons. Willie is out in the backyard "acting crazy" when his wife Linda reminds the boys that, even though Willie has failed in so many ways, he is still a human being and their father and deserves better at their hands. She says, "Attention, attention must be paid." Regardless of our condition of failure, all of us in relationships of intimacy expect basic regard; we expect to be acknowledged, taken seriously, and as a woman said, "More than noted in passing."

Caring *about* has to do with a sensitivity which enables us to stay tuned to where the lover is noting, marking, and valuing life, especially as it relates to one's person, property, and heart interests. How do you measure caring?

"So what's so special about a new hairdo?"

"It's only a car, dear, and can be straightened out."

"I could cut off my beard and you would never notice."

"If you really cared, you would call me when you will be late."

"I do care. It's just that I have a poor memory."

"It's hard to care about you when you don't care about yourself."

"If I *didn't* care, I wouldn't complain, dear."

"Some people care too much, and they get hurt."

Caring about has to do with *awareness*. If I know what is important to you, within reason I will try also to make it important to me and will pay attention so that we do not have an "out of sight, out of mind" relationship.

There is also a caring *for*. Lovers have ways of protecting, defending, and nurturing one another. Illustrations come quickly to mind: the television cliché of buckling up and locking car doors; supporting the other in his or her no-smoking or dieting program; encouraging the lover to return to school, or work, or the home when that is a nurturing thing to do; and on and on in those simple things that say I want you in my world feeling happy and loved.

Perhaps it is important here to ask how we care *for* our lover when she or he is ill. Over the years I have been surprised how often this subject appears in a couple's laundry list of "You never/You always." Some overdo and others underdo. Some lovers are resentful and petulant, scolding, "You should have listened to me and this would not have happened." Others hover and nurse until they are a smothering nuisance. Caring *for* in time of illness must be sensitively done, having to do not only with the lovers' health conditions but also with their attitudes toward illness.

The way we handle illness for ourselves and others often affects relationships globally, that is, throughout the relational sphere. There are indications that some of us welcome illness to punish others in our life system, or in order to meet the other's need to nurse and feel superior. Illness is seemingly motivated by more than micro-organisms. Illness may then become a manipulation whereby we get various other needs met, some of which may appear to be absolutely necessary for the ongoing of a particular style of relationship. Research appears even to suggest that certain kinds of heart attacks and other crippling illnesses which render a person dependent may often be locked in to unconscious perceptions of needs within the intimacy circle for one to "take care *of* or be taken care *of.*"

There is a subtle movement from "caring *for*" to "taking care *of.*" The latter—at least for me—suggests something close to a mother/child or nurse/patient relationship, and it implies considerable dependency. Times of such need occur in marriage. Yet I think it helpful to maintain a distinction between caring *for* and taking care *of,* even if that distinction sounds contrived and artificial. I make this suggestion because there is the danger of a critical loss of dignity when one is taken care *of.* If I care *for* someone, I attempt to maintain a dialogue between my highest center of human dignity and that of the other. If I take care *of,* I may tend to take charge in such a way as to cause the other to say, "What's the use? He (or she) will not pay attention to me anyway."

The reports coming out of such dependency suggest feelings of being trapped, a victim of the illness and the nurse's disposition (male or female), even to the conclusion: "I might get well if it were not for you." Indeed, it appears that people have been *kept ill* by those who need to take care *of* someone. My point is supported by numerous stories of survival of the seriously ill because someone quit blindly taking care *of* and started caring *for* a patient. There are the heartbreaking stories of persons who tell of their fear in the face of an indifferent, mindless administration of medicine and procedures, as compared to the quiet presence of a truly aware and caring person at the bedside, saying in a thousand ways, "I care *for* you."

In marriage, "take care *of* me" is a child-to-parent request or command which implies a "piggyback" or "clutch" style, which are, as we have seen, unhealthy even if some marriages can survive only in one of those modes. There are other options, perhaps the best going something like this: "I will take care *of* me, so that you may care *for* me in my need as we *both* see it."

There is another caring area—caring *with*. This has to do with the careful sharing of relationships and values within the marriage. Example: A wife complains that the husband takes little time with their nine-year-old son. Husband makes excuses. He announces them as though they are sound, valid reasons. The job is especially heavy just now. The son always seems to be busy, or has other plans every time he suggests something (perhaps twice in the last six months, and then at the last minute). Wife recalls that once after supper husband had asked son, "How would you like to go to the ball game tonight?" Son had swimming plans with his friends. Father put on his hurt look, then turned to his wife with raised eyebrows as though to say, "Well, you can't say I didn't try." After the son left the table, the argument began between husband and wife:

SHE: Don't you care about Timmy?

HE: That's a ridiculous question. You know I do.

SHE: Then show him that you care. I feel he is totally *my* responsibility. Sometimes I feel like a *single* parent. I get lonely and frightened at having to make almost all of the parent-child decisions. And I get angry with you when I have to do all the punishing. It's unfair. I am the ogre and you are Santa Claus who brings presents back from trips, then takes off to play golf with his friends.

This wife is saying care *with* me. Show that you are in this *with* me, share the fun and responsibility of parenthood, and be supportive of the extra load that, as mother, I willingly carry. Partner is needed here in the contracting and doing of the parenting team, but Lover who cares *with* is even more needed. The woman needs a man who is closer to Lover, doing the loving thing with the offspring of their love. A neighbor could take the son to the ball game. It is a different feeling for both Mother and son when Dad takes him in a caring *with* spirit for the wife and caring *about* for the son.

If these prepositional distinctions seem unnecessary, they are not. People get lost from each other. These little parts of speech point back to relational values. The wife needs real support, and the boy needs loving attention.

In summary, I want to share an acrostic that has proven helpful to people trying to clarify the care concept in marriage. Four words:

C—Suggests *carry.* I am prepared to take on your burdens when they are more than you can bear. I will get under it with you or for you. And since I care about you, I will surely carry my own weight at all times, unless I am smitten.

A—Suggests *accompany.* We are together, in concert, each one carrying his or her own part, like the voice and piano in harmony. I move with you and you with me. We pair, match, blend, and mate. We do "our own thing" *together.*

R—Suggests *resonate.* I pick up the "vibes" of your life, and try to respond on the right note. You turn on my world and I vibrate to you. We are on the same wavelength.

E—Suggests *enthuse.* From the Greek, "en Theos," it means to infuse a divine spirit. We awaken each other's life-force, and our spirits so indwell one another that we feel the movement and power of what each is about, and we share that with excitement and happiness. We breathe life into one another.

Cherish

This word is too seldom found in books about marriage. Women often seem to understand the word better than men. Yet, even among women it is too rarely used. Perhaps cherish is a word too vague, subjective, poetic—perhaps even a little too precious. In the gutsy language of pornography, the sterile nomenclature of sex manuals, and the hip talk of sock-it-to-me sex, most of the cherishables get lost; they become perishables. It may then take an enormous personal effort if we are to transcend the science and slobber of our sexual stupor. If we do not soften to death in the slow glue of Hollywood's latest love story, we can experience again something of the lyric quality of genuine love.

Despite its virtual absence in studies of marriage as a quality of relating, *cherish* appears often in the literature of love—poetry, ballads, love songs—as part of the bittersweet fantasies of lovers *in love*. Its Latin root *carus* (dear) is also the root for the French *cher*, and for our word *caress*. Dictionaries usually converge on "to hold dear" as a start toward defining *cherish*.

When we move from care to cherish in love, we have moved from the gardener's "looking *after*" to the poet's "looking *into*" with fantasy and feeling. Fantasy embellishes the beloved, and the feelings are an inspired passion that begins early to call for celebration in the genital embrace. "Looking into" has inspired poets across the ages, even before the Song of Solomon down to this present time, to sing about the lover as beautiful, virtuous, devoted, and unique. Such a person may be best described as *treasured*.

Cherish is not an empty word. Whenever I have mentioned it before an audience, the women smile knowingly. It conveys something that other words miss. It creates an ambience all its own. I have asked some of these people what the word connotes to them, and how they recognize the feeling of being cherished.

It's in the eyes—the way he looks at me. I go all soft inside. Not like jello-soft, mind you. More like honey. Yeah, cherish is all *eyes*.

Cherish is surprise. Serendipity. Beautiful surprise. Something over and beyond the call of duty. Like the way my husband made me feel when I told him I was pregnant with our fourth child and was not at all sure I wanted to be. He understood my feelings, even though he disagreed. He held me and I felt cherished.

The only time I ever *felt* cherished was in a dream just before I married (I'm divorced now). We were walking in a spring meadow, holding hands and laughing. I felt so good—innocent and free— like there was nothing to do but what we were doing, and that was the best of anything to do. It all seemed so unreal, like a scene from *Elvira Madigan*.

Cherish is a thief. It steals away reality and leaves a sweet after-taste that turns brown. So if you ever feel cherished, gargle.

Cherish is "to have and to hold." Like a swat on the bottom that says, "That's mine." (Cries from the group of MCP) She replies, "MCP, hell! I swat him more than he does me."

Cherish is a woman's word. We both got goose-pimply when you were talking about it. But she's turned on and I'm cold, scared. Sounds heavy, like poetry the way you said, and I gave that up in junior high.

I agree with whoever said cherish is all eyes, so long as she will let the hands slip in there a little bit. I think you should say more about cherish as caress.

I think to be cherished is the most perfect love there is—the way pomegranate is *the* fruit for me, the way sky means blue, and all roses are really *red* down under. Love is cherish. How does it feel? Like the ice cream I had after my tonsillectomy when I was eight.

It is poetry. I felt most cherished when my husband used to send me poems—his poems, before we were married. They were full of his feelings for me—some of them were things he has never said since. I felt really special, like NUMBER ONE, somebody like nobody else could be to him. I wish he would write me poems again.

A number of things usually emerge when people begin talking about *cherish*. (1) People have trouble sharing their feelings about feeling cherished by someone. It is very personal and private. (2) Everyone's experience with those feelings is different. Some have felt cherished but it did not last, and there was what one person called "after-taste." I am always aware of the humor associated with being cherished and am not sure whether the feelings happen that way or embarrassment causes the relieving humor. (3) The cherished feeling generally seems to associate itself with qualities of sweet, tender, often erotic, acceptance. (4) That acceptance is not only unconditional, it is without comparison: "I'm NUMBER ONE." Most of us yearn for this, to be preeminent in someone's life, the most important other. Second-among-equals for lovers is not possible for most of us. We want to be *first,* among no other equals. (5) For others, cherish suggests feelings of being adored, revered, prized, and esteemed, all words that express an elevation of feelings to the point at which one seems to be of extraordinary worth. If it is not parasitic or idolatrous, having such feelings as a gift of another's love can be a beautiful and enhancing thing; but to be healthy and effective, it must be mutually given, each to the other.

My wife recalls as a little girl asking her Aunt Marjorie why she polished her silver. "Does it make it taste better?" Marjorie laughed and said, "No, I guess I just like to see it shine." There is something about cherishing that is like that; it is not so much practical as caring, more to see the glow and feel the warmth of such awareness and recognition of the other.

If cherish is a woman's word, men should pay attention, because we need to know what the feeling is that they so enjoy, and because we need it too. Perhaps men shy away from it because of its quality of tenderness. Perhaps cherish suggests to some men an absolute commitment that makes them feel trapped. Perhaps it is the *intensity* of the feeling which cherish elicits that troubles us. Perhaps it is none of these, and we are simply unfamiliar with the word as a working word of love. After all, how many words do we use for love in our man's world? Hardly any at all.

I believe in both the power and the magic of words. If communication is talking and touching, we need something like words to get our message across. Cherish is one of those words. It is a heart word. Like a magnet it can gather new, tender feelings in us, perhaps feelings just taking shape, creating enough energy for us to fantasize what we may offer our lover as a gift of *I cherish you.* Such a fantasy or daydream may begin just now as an exercise in learning to give the gifts of cherishing. It is to be hoped that such a beginning would lead to greater spontaneity, so that at the heart of the relationship is the frequent, generous giving of such a love. What causes your lover to feel most cherished?

Celebrate

Life should be decorated throughout with celebrative events. Most of us manage to pay attention to the festivals: rites of faith, such as baptism or bar mitzvah; to national and religious holidays; and even to unique anniversaries, such as the day we opened our own shop or a homecoming from war. We are likely to continue family traditions on certain special days, such as Halloween, Mother's Day, or the reunion trade-offs on Thanksgiving and Christmas, where we often eat and drink too much, play "competition"—the family game of most-is-best, using pieces called jobs, money, cars, boats, and children. We may attend in order to avoid being talked about, although being present does not seem to stop some families.

These are often occasions for getting off the wagon, dumping the diet, and generally inviting indiscretions of all sorts. I am still intrigued by reports of what goes on at many family reunions, and who did or said what to whom—all in the name of "just trying to relax and have a little fun." Incidents range all the way from malicious insult to incest. There are, of course, gatherings of family loved ones which are joyful and rejuvenating, but there seem to be all too many of the other kind.

Love finds its character in caring, its heart in cherishing, and its soul in celebrating. Soul is psyche, spirit—the living, breathing essence of personhood. Celebration is the great integrating power of every human being who cries, "All is well!" Celebration emerges out of and brings with it a feeling that *life is good,* which is our noblest human response.

Celebration may be attempted at times other than when life is good, when life in fact is not good, or is being experienced that way. These are celebrations of memory (how it was) or of fantasy (how it might be).

Genuine celebration of the soul is ecstasy (to stand outside of), when we are apt to feel transported, lost, out of this world. Alexander Lowen, in his book *Pleasure,* cautions that real ecstasy is not painful, but exquisitely pleasurable. Creative celebration gives wings for soaring, from which we are brought back to earth better grounded, with new feelings of buoyancy and hope, and a clearer resolve about the intent and direction of our lives. The spirit expands and dreams, makes space for breathing and motion, flexes body and mind, and perhaps for an interval slips out of time and feels at home with the universe. These can be quiet moments. They often come privately for me when I am sailing, or writing a poem, or just lying in the backyard watching the woodpeckers and squirrels flitting in the high-vaulted treetops of oak, ash, and maple. Right now the breeze is playful; the sun is quite warm and flecking through the branches. There is a spirit of peaceful celebration: *life is good!*

Destructive celebration, historically called orgy, deadens the spirit, is at most distractive and escapist, tends to become an end in itself, and fails to equip us for living. It cannot be called celebration at all. It is a defamation of the human spirit and of any "life is good" concept. It more often seems to say, "Life is so bad, but this is the only way we are able to survive."

Some people live life with such a vengeance that they are left jaded and depressed, so that a quick blast of narcosis from alcohol or other drugs seems like the easiest and surest way out of the pit. But they never get out; nothing changes except their awareness. Things look different, but they aren't, and later they pick up the new day with the same old fatigue and disenchantment. It is a winding down, grinding down way to do life. The only hope is some real attempt at creative celebration.

Love thrives on celebration. Love may survive without celebration; it may persist in the face of enormous calamity like scrub pines in poor soil, against ferocious winds at the edge of a rocky tree line. But love flourishes best in creative celebration.

Lovers celebrate their love. We do this best by celebrating ourselves as aware, autonomous persons and by celebrating the other in caring and cherishing ways which make both of us feel loved, stimulated, and enjoyed. Such times, in marriage, can come in a moment and for the taking if we are awake and our spirits not eroded. But such times might better also be *planned* as something to look forward to, and to make sure that those times of respite, abandonment, and relaxed aliveness are a vital part of our way of life and not just chance happenings. Some couples find it helpful to spend *at least* one hour together each day or evening, at least one major four-hour period every weekend, a long weekend once a quarter, and half of the family's vacation time if they have children. Separate vacations are sometimes appropriate. These time frames seem necessary to the health of a married relationship. A couple can build in more time as it is available.

Yet, couples still find excuses: there isn't enough money; we can't find baby-sitters; time is our problem; and—worst of all—there just doesn't seem to be that much to say to each other. We usually do what we *want* to do. If people take their children everywhere they go, spend every weekend with his folks or hers, only go out with other couples, and reduce all fun time together to "what does it cost?" I assume that they really do not enjoy each other very much, and in some real way they want to avoid each other and avoid facing that fact.

My fear is that we have not yet understood the place and need for celebration in marriage. We have had work models, children models, religious models, survival models, success models, etc. Yet, in all of these there has been little room for celebration. Small successes, such as a child bringing home good grades, are still reported to me as being ignored by parents, or dismissed with, "That's what you are supposed to do." There may not even be a word of congratulations, much less genuine praise and some simple celebration. Our models may include going out, having friends or relatives over, or a party now and then, but I am speaking for a spirit, an attitude that *demands* that life and love be celebrated. The parties and going out may very well be celebrations. The most important thing is that we enjoy these events, that they leave us feeling "up" and refreshed, and as a couple they help us to feel closer rather than alienated, more loved than rejected.

Assuming that celebration is a good thing, that every couple needs it, and it really is fun, how do we do it? Again, it is important to remember *privacy, intimacy, community,* and *transcendence* as modes or spheres in which we experience the exhilarating exclamation: *life is good.* Without this movement through the four basic areas of human response, it is difficult if not impossible to have a genuinely celebrative spirit in a marriage. A subtle and exciting interaction occurs between and among all four.

There are two basic movements through them. One, I call the *crescendo movement* when a life-is-good affirmation begins with self, moves into at least one truly intimate relationship, and outward to others with whom life is truly good, climaxing in a declaration to the universe that in this moment living is good. The second is what I call a *movement of grace.* Celebration may occur in one area when it is impossible for us to feel that life is good in another. This has been one of the hallmarks of every good religion; it gives us *passage*—albeit not free passage, as Bonhoeffer warns us about cheap grace—out of the death sphere into the life sphere. It is opting for life rather than death. This is resurrection.

The Hebrew-Christian literature is filled with examples of such grace. This movement of grace may be the chief thing that keeps us sane. When life in the private sphere seems overwhelmingly tragic, or absurdly comic at best, and there is little spirit for celebration, another who lives close to our world, who knows and loves us, is often able to redeem that pain with love and call us into celebration. The "community of the believers" in every faith is for many a support fellowship whose love embraces with such tenderness and assurance that life there becomes good. Self-worth may be uncovered in that company; perhaps a relationship of intimacy is created so that love makes a home in us, and in the most transcending ways life becomes fulfilling, meaningful, and celebrative. Perhaps it is not over against or in spite of, but *because* of the work of religious communities that we have discovered in more recent years that the so-called secular communities are also able to give meaning and celebration to life. Regardless, it would appear that celebration must occur throughout the life range for one to make a full and vital commitment to life as essentially and ultimately good.

The acceptance of death as more than "the bitter end" depends upon some transcending celebration of the fundamental glory of all creation and my small place in it. Despite the childlikeness of such sentiment, I do share life with the butterfly who has but one day, with that fantastic whippoorwill outside my window this moment, and with the extravagant cascade of roses dying upon the fence, and I celebrate. Life is *good.* Nature is capricious and violent. Men, women, and children can be cruel, often are, and spoil life for themselves and others. But still, *life* is good. It is a worthy human task to help more people experience it that way. Even though history is strewn with corpses of those who died in our grisly battles over definitions of the good life, or the good person, I believe that we are further along in our struggle with people and the environment toward the celebration of life as fundamentally good for the whole creation.

The way we celebrate depends on our origins, values, tastes, life-style, etc. The merger of two personal patterns of celebration in marriage can be exciting. It may also create problems, especially if values are threatened or feelings abused by embarrassment or disappointment during those celebrative events. For example, the community and transcendence spheres can cause conflict in marriage, especially as they relate to loyalty and commitment expected by national origin, familial, racial, or religious groups. The celebrations of "life is good" can be radically different, for example, in Christian and Jewish homes, or for that matter, among the various branches of either. It is only in acknowledging the best of each that the couple can reap the rewards of entering into each other's celebrations.

The central concern of this section is celebrating love *in marriage.* We have seen that a basic understanding of celebration is that it is a joyous statement that life is good. In marriage it is, "Life *with you* is good." Definitional statements are difficult to make since each couple's model is unique and not apt to fit any stereotype. Still, there are at least three universals to be noted.

Celebrative love in marriage is characterized for most couples as *sensual, sexual,* and *genital,* as expressed most profoundly in intimacy arising out of a healthy privacy, and finding expression in both community and transcendence. Members of the couple's community will see *muted* expressions of their sensual, sexual, and genital celebration and know that it is not a neutered marriage. A couple's life-statement as to the meaning of marriage (transcendence) may also reflect the sensual, sexual, and genital celebration in the sphere of intimacy. Couples reflect the value they place on their uniqueness as man and woman, their respect for that uniqueness, and pleasure in it. This is evidenced in their behavior, be it in an elevator or a church. It says, "Notice how they talk and touch, how they support and enhance each other's sexual identity. They like being a man and a woman, and they like it together even more. It's a good bet they know something about making love." Rather than, "They never really talk and touch. They fight like a cobra and a mongoose. If either were the last man or woman in the world, you could cancel the next generation."

Sensuality

The sensual celebration of love has to do with the five senses and our ability to use them to experience and communicate pleasurable feelings for ourselves and our lover. It is, therefore, imperative that intimacy permit a maximizing of the sensual experience—that is, our ability to stimulate the five senses in a play-event in which we see, touch, hear, smell, and taste that which enhances the pleasure factors of closeness. Body pleasure is essential to emotional health and ego fulfillment. We must play and feel good if we are to work and be well.

Time, place, and *energy* are primary components for setting the stage for most celebrations. Unless we make time, prepare an environment, and have the energy for meeting, there is little likelihood of much happening. Giving another our *time* is a precious gift. It is probably the thing most often requested by a husband or wife in marriage counseling. To offer time in a place in which we are most apt to meet at a depth is—after years of the cliché "back-seat sex"—an added bonus. But to give time in a supportive environment when my energy is still flowing strong focuses these three principal elements for the greatest possibility of pleasure. However, sensuous exchanges may occur in many different places, at odd times, and at various levels of energy. Part of the nature of celebration is "breakout"—celebrating when and where least expected, which can be the crucial factor in certain celebrative events. A couple reported driving home exhausted from an extended meeting of intercity agencies in a great metropolitan center at the height of the racial struggles. Passing a beautiful reflection pool and fountain, they stopped and went splashing through the sparkling water at one o'clock in the morning like children chasing a Pied Piper, finally falling down and rolling around in the water until both were soaked through and exhausted from tickling and laughing. Tempted to make love under the dogwoods, they restrained themselves, because of the traffic, and went home in their sopping clothes to the privacy of their own backyard lawn.

Dr. Comfort's book, *The Joy of Sex,* and its sequel are full of sensual delights which titillate and turn-on. However, there are many body pleasures which need not lead to intercourse, which, perhaps, in fact *should* not. A complaint often heard in marriage counseling is that simple body pleasures too frequently serve merely for genital arousal and are not enjoyed *for themselves.* When a wife frets that when she turned the garden hose on her husband in the yard one day and he practically raped her, and he does not deny it, the problem need not be "get even" or "latent hostility," but simply the man's *inability to play.* He might have grabbed the hose and doused her. Instead, it served only as a potent signal or stimulant for intercourse, against her will.

As a little film classic so well portrays, a couple eating an orange together—all the way from examining the fruit to licking juice from the fingers—can be a feast for eyes, nose, mouth, hands, and ears (Mmmm!). Only the limits of imagination can exhaust the list of possibilities available to the individual and the couple in giving the body a sensory treat. The body likes to *move* (even more than it likes weights, push-ups, etc.): dancing, walking, running, swimming. It likes *aromas*—from its own and the Lover's body essence to exotic perfumes, as well as nature's own fragrances in flowers, fresh-cut grass, bread, cheese, sea spray, a wooded glen, a plowed field, October in an apple barn, farmyard odors, pine resin, and on forever. The body likes *sounds*—from a baby's tiny sleeping sounds to the roar of mountain streams. It likes *touching* all sorts of textures and can distinguish a grain of sand or an eyelash; and it likes *being touched*—warm and cool, soft and hard, tapping and stroking. The body likes to *taste:* the tongue is an army of little samplers. The variety and harmony of flavors are parts of any "gourmet's delight." It likes to *see*—shape, form, substance, color, size, distance, the calm, the storm, muted darkness, sunrise, moon glow, other eyes, the human body, fantasy.

A body experience which is very in-body and terribly sensual is fantasy. Like a dream, a fantasy can enliven the body so that it believes what it is "seeing and experiencing" in the fantasy.

Fantasy

The next time you travel a boring turnpike with little traffic, in fantasy imagine yourself *outside* the car:

feel with your hands the gravel at the edge of the pavement, the difference in temperature from pavement to earth, the prickly touch of mowed grass stubble on the road shoulders, the bark of trees, and the sharp barb of wire fencing;

smell the creosote on the posts, the musky under-bridge odor, the fruit-tree blossoms, the dead animal alongside, the clover (and honey, miles away);

hear drones, buzzes, blops, whistles, songs, and whooshes of things seen as in a silent movie from your car;

stretch all the senses, bathing your body inside and out as you become totally immersed in the outside environment;

and after fifteen minutes you may emerge from this "trip" refreshed, amused with the distraction, and delighted.

Fantasy

Using individual sets of earphones, listen with your Lover to a recording, something long enough to create its mood. When the record is well under way, take off the earphones and experiment with letting your awareness move back and forth from "inside to outside" and return: eyes open, eyes closed, touching, not touching, etc. Something *else,* something *more* happens to the senses when you take off the phones and are greeted by silence, or the sound of crickets, or the city, or your own whispers. It is different than just turning off the stereo. The earphones transport you. It is as though the room has not participated in the sound—a deaf man could not have touched the walls and felt the vibrations. To come out of the music, into the room, and back again (with the sounds still in your head) creates shifting sensations in the mind combined with a very different meeting outside, like stepping out of the shower into the waiting arms of your Lover.

Fantasy

Just upon going to bed, close your eyes and imagine yourself naked in a beautiful pool in which you are assured of privacy. Surround the pool with exotica—flowers, birds, statuary, music, trees, and fish in the water. Move in the water in ways that will maximize the body experience, emphasizing the water event. If you do not swim or if you fear water, all the more reason to enjoy the fantasy. Dive to the bottom of the pool and feel the water temperature and the currents change. See the beautiful fish and electric eels. Hear the music under water. Touch the cool rocks and white sand. Be there! Caress your body with your hands. Enjoy. Drift off to sleep.

These fantasies allow the imagination to create sensations which actually enliven and accent body awareness. We know the power of dreams to terrify, move to tears, or bring to sexual orgasm. Fantasy is also able to generate body feelings, have extraordinary strength to stir or quiet the body systems and deeply touch the psyche, the central control agency, of the whole person. Fantasy is one of numerous ways to give ourselves sensuous, celebrative moments, and all that is required is a willing imagination.

Lovers play "do you remember?" games recalling body feelings:

That was the coldest water we ever swam in.

I can still taste the champagne.

The only sounds I remember are his singing and your saying, "I do."

The flowers at Kensington smelled like heaven.

Lovers can also do fantasy *together* in concert, mixing their impressions and feelings as though they were jointly telling a story. This way you share imaginary gifts that are pleasurable and stimulating. The input may both surprise you and support your own reverie. It will undoubtedly reveal where your mind plays and how well your body responds to your pictures and those of your lover.

Sexual

It is easy to see how at least two of the above fantasies might become explicitly sexual. That's fine. I have divided celebration into sensual, sexual, and genital experiences in order to say a number of things, among them being that the first (sensual) or second (sexual) need not lead to the third (genital). Such a statement may seem unnecessary, but some people still avoid the pure experience of the five senses, or avoid being in the world as a sexual adult because something or someone has taught them to be afraid of good feelings, since those feelings frequently lead to "something worse," or a vague "you know what," or boldly—intercourse.

The noblest human posture demands that we be in the world as sexual adults. To deny our sexuality is to cripple the whole person. "Male and female created He them" is one of the oldest poetic ascriptions to form, figure, and life on this planet. In these sexual crowns are reflected other dualities: sun–moon, Yin–Yang, light–dark, soft–hard, poetic–rational, etc. We share with all of the more sophisticated life-forms the absolute inter-dependability of male and female. In most instances *the growing apart and coming together* represent the thrust of the total life effort—the central, organizing principle of plant and creature.

Having recently survived our "unisex period," when long hair and jeans were everywhere, and the muting of sexual distinctions seemed to represent a conscious effort to confuse the sexual stereotypes, it is important to note two things: (1) sexual stereotypes are an attempt to maintain custodial and functional differences (men do this, women do that), while (2) at the same time, true stereotypes seriously threaten the marvelous gifts of our uniqueness. We are all male *and* female. There is a point in gestation when every embryo is a unisex. Then each appears clearly female and would emerge with female genitalia, except when appropriately a chromosome carrying the genetic code signals "boy" and the male hormone, testosterone, commands that the basic female embryo become male. Afterwards, it is the preponderance of male or female hormones which continues to support the sexual difference and their functions. Hence, *anything*—symbol or function—which we call male or female is potentially or actually present in *both* man and woman.

Here is a little puzzle by which we can sift out the "heavy weight" in sexual stereotyping. The following are twenty characteristics which our culture usually assigns to male and female. Place a number by each word in both columns as you feel you possess that characteristic, giving the following weight to each word: Strong—4; Mild—3; Weak—2; Absent—0. Then total each column.

Male	**Female**
aggressive	affectionate
ambitious	compassionate
assertive	gentle
athletic	loving toward children
competitive	loyal
dominant	sensitive to others
forceful	sympathetic
independent	tender
self-reliant	understanding
willing to take a stand	warm
Total _____	Total _____

The best balanced scores are those which fall between 35 to 40 in *each* column; that is, when a person is close to strong in all of the above characteristics. For a man to score weak to zero in most of the words under *Female* is to make him a male stereotype heavyweight, and weak to absent in at least ten of the most critically human factors of character and personality. The reverse is true for females. If we accept the notion that there are custodial and functional differences between male and female, and that these differences survive in the best interests of the human race, we must at the same time insist that wherever possible both sexes share in the expression of the fascinating versatility of human creatures in all the communication systems of our interaction. If I as a male do not participate in what is called a female quality, I am impoverished in my own experience and crippled in my expression. "No man is an island unto himself"— flowing through every cell of his being is the awesome female hormone, progesterone, imprinting man with woman.

One of Carl Jung's major intellectual efforts was to track down and understand what he called the *anima* (feminine) and the *animus* (masculine). He suggested that the *outward* face that we present be called the *persona* (the mask). The *inward* face for males is the female *anima,* while for females it is the male *animus.* Jung believed that to be psychologically healthy, men must express their feminine side, and women their masculine. Two excellent books on this subject have been written by Robert A. Johnson. One is titled *She,* and the other is *He.* Using the great, classic myths and mythical figures, Johnson has movingly described the complex workings of what we think of as the mystery of human sexuality in man and woman.

Perhaps one of the most helpful studies in this area is June Singer's *Androgyny,* in which she explores the concept of androgyny as it "involves recognizing the eternal flux of these opposing energies" best understood by most of us as masculine and feminine. Comprehending and celebrating the presence of these dualities helps us to become whole creatures and also gives unity to our symbolic and mythic world.

We are left, then, with the considerable problems of *focus* and *balance* in distinguishing the sexes. *Focus* is perhaps best described as the ability of males convincingly to celebrate being men, and females convincingly to celebrate being women. Neither sex will feel neutered so long as the other is convinced, and each is fulfilled as man or woman in the presence of the other. For men and women to feel fulfilled at a given level of interaction is perhaps the simplest test of mature adult sexuality. This *fulfillment* has to do with being perceived, accepted, understood, and appreciated as a man, or as a woman, by the opposite sex. It may be a simple exchange with a clerk in a store, when somehow the "essence" of one's sexuality is received/exchanged, and we are known in the moment as man or woman.

Needless to say, such perceptions do not emerge from vacuums. For a man to say to himself in the above illustration, "Now, there's a woman!" means that he has automatically processed millions of signals from his environment as to what a woman is. Ignoring the obviously freakish exception, when a man or woman with distorted notions of the nature of man and woman meet and affirm each other, I believe that we must simply trust this process of a man feeling like man (fulfilled) in woman's presence (and vice versa) as the best criterion we have for adult sexuality. For it is in this exchange that the business which a man and a woman have with each other will get done—physically, spiritually, psychologically, intellectually, and socially. The relationship is constantly evolving, and man and woman are discovering what each needs of the other and what each can give in order to put together the most fulfilling relationship possible for both, and integrally for the human family.

"Orders from on high" less and less affect what men and women must "get done" together. God, church, and tribe have rapidly lost voice in terms of dictating the nature of the male-female exchange. One new direction now is coming from the state, which—in its ongoing process of self-deification—conditions our prerogatives in the most personal and intimate spheres of life. For example, the day may come when a couple must obtain a license in order to have a child, just as India has already begun enforcing sterility after a person has mothered or fathered a third child. The focus of sexuality today has to do with the ability of men and women to realize their greatest possible fulfillment now at this point in the journey of the sexes, as men and women meet and celebrate themselves and one another.

Balance is the ability of men and women to so order their relationships as to maximize the variety and energy of their ways of being with each other. For example, it would be sad if a woman had always to be with a man in one mode—traditionally subordinate— and the man had always to be strong and in charge; so that even when he is ill, he must deny it and tell his family to "clear out." Or, contrarily, each agrees it is alright to react differently, so that a strong man becomes helpless, needing a nurse. Or a weak woman makes a show of strength by remaining on her feet even though quite ill, thus receiving the admiration of her family while swallowing her anger at not being "allowed" to be sick. Balance in the sexes means that each has, owns, and uses the qualities ascribed to both, and they celebrate this abundance in one another. There is no fear of being castrated or raped, no unhealthy competition for the position of "top dog," and no need for the man to put the woman down in order to feel like a man, or for the woman to be absurdly careful of the man's fragile ego. "Adam and Eve" seek a fulfilling balance.

We are presently engaged in a dialogue in this country and in many other parts of the world in which the *focus* and *balance* elements of the man-woman encounter are the poles around which are gathering the changing identities of each sex. As women discover their needs and the needs of men in the twentieth century, they attempt to gather resources necessary for meeting those needs. Educated, articulate, talented women see no reason to accept financial dependence. In an overcrowded world, most women will not make motherhood the only significant task of their adult years. With the new freedom of the contraceptive, women are also liberated from their sexual prisons and given a new *genital* reality—they can and should enjoy sexual satisfaction and fulfillment. They can decide whether or not to bear children on the basis of their own personal data for making the choice, and not on the basis of a societal overlay regarding this decision. This separates childbearing from sexual-genital pleasure.

In the midst of these enormous changes, women are trying to focus on the ancient question of "Who am I?" It is also true for men who—faced with the "more is better" value assumptions of our culture which impose the more work, more money, more *things* merry-go-round—often find themselves depressed with jaded values and feelings, and terrible bitterness.

The "Who are *we*?" question then emerges as men and women struggle for individual and corporate identity. They are asking questions that have no automatic answers, and some drive right to the roots of the ultimate meaning of man and woman: Are we different except for the organs which function for pleasure and propagation?

Any attempt to say "yes" to this question has to do with focus: how *else* do man and woman differ? Even if we *assume* that men and women are custodians of certain values or human resources which are clearly designated male and female, there is no evidence to prove that these are hormonally decided. Primary and secondary sexual characteristics—genitals, breasts, hair, voice, etc.—are hormonal effects. There is no clear evidence that women are assigned moral, psychological, or emotional custodialship. Society may do that, but, as we have said, that means that man and woman are then denied certain rights more theirs as human beings than theirs as a sex. A *person* needs to be able to cry, regardless of what little boys are supposed to do. A *person* needs to show affection, to embrace and kiss, regardless of what a cold father and a warm mother might have taught. A *person* needs to be intuitive regardless of the fact that women had to be because men told them they were not rational creatures and to act so would be to appear masculine. A *person* needs to be assertive, strong, and autonomous. A *person* raises children regardless of what Mommie says and what Daddy does.

It is clear that being male or female is at the heart of one's identity, but we have lost much of our *humanity* in trying to protect our sexual roles (Mother and Father), our sexual property (virgins), our sexual lust (the body beautiful), etc. A "total woman" concept denigrates woman if she, as *person,* is seduced while seducing "her man." The "total woman" is a partial person. She manages to capture and keep her man only at the price of her pride, and at the expense of her own autonomous ego. Her life is meaningful only in the catering and pandering posture of servant and sex object. It is a prostitution of all that might be called holy in personhood and an adulteration of the sexual partnership of equality. The woman's selfhood is lost in the pampering and babying of her greedy and consumptive man. The assumption that her man will return the favors is an afterthought, attached as a hope or dream, but never a part of a contract between the man and woman to get each other deeply loved and cared for. Robert A. Johnson's book, *She,* tells of Amazon women who cut off a breast in order to handle the bow and arrow with greater accuracy. The opposite in a "total woman" complex might suggest that women grow a third breast because "her man" likes the other two so well. "Total-woman" females have slain the *animus* and survive as half-persons, and only a total-man, oblivious to his *anima,* or an effeminate total-woman-sort-of-male could tolerate her truckling, menial, baby-doll ways. A male chauvinist stud, whose focus is total-genital, or a Milquetoast who needs the total woman to inspire and erect him, will love her. Men who want a whole-woman friend, partner, and lover will not.

The *new* focus of sexual differences may then have to do with helping each other realize and express man in woman and woman in man. Perhaps a woman's greatest gift to man is to call for his *anima* and give him a supportive environment in which to experience his own femaleness. Only a whole woman is secure enough to permit the man to express his feminine side, and only a whole man, who trusts his manhood, is free and secure enough to give expression to the feminine side of him. Of course, the opposite is true: perhaps the man's greatest gift to the woman is to call for and support the expression of her *animus,* her masculine side, and thus encourage her to be a *whole person* rather than total woman. We should be striving for a whole-person concept rather than some total-gender concept which leaves a man and a woman looking strained, overstated, and ridiculous in their relationship.

Perhaps, in fairness, we should say that women seem more willing to let men express their *anima* than men seem willing to let women express their *animus.* A man may be able to rise to the contest among other men and be beaten because his opponent was "a better man," but the same man may be horrified at the sight of a woman "on the playing field" of sports, office, or bed. She must not be assertive, strong, competitive, or initiating. Nothing is more humiliating for some men than to be beaten by a woman. Even if the woman is reassuring and supportive, the man is likely to be suspicious and jealous. He wants her off his field (unless she is his sexy cheerleader with pom-poms), out of his office (except as his playful and seductive maid), and out of his bed (other than as playboy bunny for his pleasure and satisfaction). The twin to this sort of male is the anxious man who feels he is not quite making it as a man unless he can give "his woman" an orgasm, perhaps multiple orgasms, *every* time.

Genital

Most adults desire genital union. Most of us strive for this and are incomplete and unfulfilled without it. All male-female meetings of consequence are conditioned by a fantasy, the memory, or an anticipation of genital intercourse. This does not mean that every time men and women meet, they are consciously preoccupied with genital union; but they are at least conditioned by what is imagined or experienced genitally with that person or some other.

The possibility of genital union significantly affects what transpires between a man and a woman. The person before you is not a neuter. He or she is either man or woman. That makes a difference, regardless of the conversation or the activity shared. That "difference" is a numinous, erotic field of "woman" or "man" generated out of the entire human experience. Central to that field is the possibility of genital union in fantasy, memory, or anticipation: if not now, sometime; if not here, somewhere; and if not with this person, then with someone.

More universally than anything else, genital intercourse fulfills man and woman. It represents symbolically and delivers substantively our deepest sense of wholeness and health. It is the ground of pleasure and the body's surest ecstasy. It is, then, not unlikely that meetings between men and women become "charged" in ways in which meetings with the same sex, for heterosexuals, are not. It is because quite explicitly—or buried somewhere in the psyche as the merest hint, like jasmine—there is the *promise* of the ultimate human bond, man and woman living in genital embrace.

In addition to foreplay and afterplay, genital union between loving adults has at least three other distinct aspects. They are *penetration, synthesis,* and *orgasm.*

1. The moment of *penetration* signals genital union, the unique conditioning fantasy in male-female meeting. It is in that moment that man convincingly crosses the threshold into woman. She welcomes him with abandon. There is an exultant *sense of arrival.* Every touch, look, word, and maneuver has led to this homecoming of the sexes. Even in the mythology of the virgin, it is the moment when girl becomes woman, boy becomes man, as though penetration symbolically opens the way and sets free. It is transitional—a rite of sexual passage. More profoundly, it is the *meeting* of man and woman.

2. *Synthesis,* if it occurs, transcends even this union. After penetration there comes the shifting, moving, and lifting; the warm mouth of the vagina receiving every stroke of the penis with an intuition and a *yes* followed by the slightest inflection of muscle; *no,* then a new turning, rolling, slipping toward synthesis, when the two become one and each the other. There is at the center a waiting in the psychic roots of all our genital awareness for this mystical union. The man is buried in the woman. She envelops him. They say their words, meaningless, precious, reassuring. They lift, hover, and sail. They whimper and battle, bathe and caress toward the melding, in the clutching, tangled mix of fire, gasping breath, and pelvic pounding, the air turbulent with a sweet, riding home alone, together, one. And the rhythm of that ride is the fine meter of all their meeting.

3. *Orgasm* is central to what our nature is about in genital intercourse. Anyone who settles for less needs to understand that is exactly what has happened. There are exciting trips in which "getting there is half the fun," but only *half.* The so-called trip is about *arriving.* So is orgasm. Without it there is often painful and frustrating disappointment. When lovers know what arriving is like, they will only reluctantly continue to settle for *"half* the fun of getting there."

We finally come down to whether or not a man and woman can experience that most abandoned moment of all, when the body and psyche, risking everything, explode into each other's awareness with breathless expansion and release, and with gratitude for "such a gift as this between us, for me and for you." Afterwards follows a beautiful tranquillity when the subtlest messages of love and tenderness are exchanged, and then sleep.

There is always a danger of getting caught in the spell being woven by those who tout orgasm as worthy of worship. Such evangelism can be expected as we emerge from our Puritan denialism and the male chauvinist imperialism which has featured a hegemony over women. However, nature's balance simply asserts a genital communion between men and women in which they should expect to achieve orgasm. When the body is allowed to move naturally and instinctively to its logical end, orgasm should occur. If this does not happen, we have blocked it.

As the social mores change and we take more seriously our sexual-genital needs and rights, men and women are paying more attention to what happens during lovemaking and intercourse. The pleasure experience and conception are clearly separate. Pleasure outlives the possibility of conception. Conception is necessary for survival of the race. This is surely also true of *pleasure*. Orgasm is intense pleasure, and there need not be either the intention or possibility of conception.

The Masters and Johnson research has not only mapped the sexual-genital response, but it also has called attention to the experience in ways that have caused us to accept, discuss, and improve that experience with our lover. There has been a deluge of books, magazine articles, workshops, and lectures on the subject. While most couples reject becoming sexual athletes, they are genuinely interested in how their bodies and psyches can be stimulated toward sensual, sexual, genital enrichment and gratification.

Perhaps it needs to be said that each one is responsible for his or her own orgasm. For years we heard that the man "gave" the woman her orgasm. This is impossible. With help from our partner, we "get" our own. Each person knows what needs to happen in order for orgasm to occur; so we must accept the fact that unless we know what we are about and can bring together the right feelings, no climax will occur regardless of our lover's intention for us. It is up to you to invite and create the kind of play most conducive to climax.

The ease and success of the new sex therapies testify to the body's abilities to find its own way and reach its end. Without making absolute promises for universal success, we can say that it is now usually possible for healthy adults to achieve orgasm. Sexually unsatisfied men and women owe it to themselves to investigate the possibility of rectifying the condition. The odds for recovery are too good not to try.

Friends, partners, and lovers arriving at this point together in their relationship are now simply invited to create an environment in which they can best express their love and give pleasure to one another. In this giving we receive loving. While this is not a "how-to" sex manual, my suggestions to couples usually include something like this:

Although lovemaking may occur in many different places, the

bedroom is where most of us expect it to happen. Let it reflect your taste at its most inviting and satisfying. Drab, cramped, and cluttered bedrooms with ironing boards, desks, sewing machines, and other foreign objects are disheartening. A dull, uninspired room is insulting to your own feelings. A cutesy "boudoir" littered with kewpie dolls, lacy pillows, knickknacks, and plastic flowers may not do much for the five senses. Dress the room to invite and stimulate.

Soft light, music, throw rugs and cushions for variety from bad beds and thin carpets, favorite pictures and fragrances, the right clothes or no clothes can enhance the event. There should be enough time uninterrupted by phones or children. Good talk, touching, bathing, and massaging with body lotions can be pleasant and fun. Women sometime complain that men do not talk and touch enough, so that women feel rushed and cheated of the closeness they desire. A variety of positions for intercourse, freedom for sexual fantasy, intimate language, and little, private games are appropriate. Time, place, and energy to feel loved and experience orgasm are the simple needs to be met. What both want is what should occur. We create our own unique play. *Find* each other and say so with talk and touch.

This experience is so important to marriage that it is hard to imagine too much preparation for lovemaking. Often our preparation for lesser events is more elaborate and consuming. Social parties are better arranged than our private, love party. Our energy and care are better given to neighbors than to our mates, Making love has a special priority in marriage, and it deserves our best effort. The love experience permeates the entire marriage and colors every nuance. We must protect this time together and frequently discuss how we might improve the experience. Few exchanges will have greater impact upon the quality of the marriage than this personal and intimate expression of what it means to be man and woman together.

CREATING THE 6 FUTURE TOGETHER

I just live from day to day," said the young wife. "My husband refuses to share any of his plans with me, if he has any. There is nothing to look forward to. The other day at his sister's house—she has a three-week-old little girl—he had the gall to say, 'Why don't we have another baby?'" I just looked at him and laughed. "That's as close as we ever get to planning. The two we have were accidents. Our whole life is just one accident after another."

Why Some Couples Do Not Plan Together

Many couples refuse to plan together. Understanding why we refuse is the first step toward changing the situation. We must consciously set goals and strategize those goals toward fruition. Following are a few reasons why couples refuse to plan. It may be helpful to see if any of these block your planning.

1. *A need to control.* One may need to maintain control of the marriage generally or of some specific aspect central to the relationship, such as sex or money. The mate's controlling influence then permeates the marriage, so as to neutralize the other's input in important matters. The neglected spouse simply resigns from the process, and by default, power and control are retained by the other.

Questions: Which of us holds the power in this marriage? Why? How is that power used to nurture and enhance our lives together and to mold the future?

2. *Reluctant mate.* One may be only "half in the marriage." To plan or dream together is to imply a commitment beyond where a spouse is or wants to be. Half-attention responses, such as "Yeah, we'll have to talk about that sometime," often reflect the spouse's attitude, especially if the issue is important and clearly needs attention. Discussions that require long-term planning will be consistently avoided by the reluctant mate. Questions: Do we constantly shelve the big issues? Why?

3. *Deprecation of the mate.* "You are terrible at planning or making decisions, so I have to do it." The mask for such arrogance of power is usually, "Look at the time you . . ." and some painful failure is cited. One man shyly attempted to begin his journey toward autonomy when he asked his mothering wife, "Well, I decided to marry you, didn't I?" He was immediately sabotaged with her retort, "No, dear, I decided that you would marry me if I asked you to." Questions: Is one of us made to feel put down as inadequate for the decision-making processes of our marriage? Which of us? Why?

4. *Feelings of inferiority.* A wife says she wants her husband to make the decisions and do the planning because she does not trust her own judgment. In what matters? Under what circumstances? In discussion with whom? Some such women plan and decide quite well when the husband is absent. They do well with their own routine, household concerns, in emergencies, or at the club. Deference may have more to do with one's mate than with the real ability of the one opting out. For example, some men need dependent and weak wives in order to feel like men. If there are honest feelings of inferiority, these should be given attention rather than allow them to cripple the planning process. Questions: Does one of us appear to be or feel inferior? What are *we* doing about such feelings?

5. *Fear of results.* One may actually fear suggesting that the planning be shared. Humiliation, the "silent treatment," dumping ("Okay, if you're so smart, go do it."), or even physical abuse may counsel one to leave the subject alone. Or perhaps there is the fear that, if the thing fails, one will blame the other. Questions: Do we cop out by blaming each other? What is the *real* issue here?

6. *Refusal of responsibility.* One mate simply does not like being responsible. To follow is safer and more comfortable. The exceptions among such persons are interesting. One may make little decisions and shun the big ones, even in the face of proof that the little ones are more important. Questions: Is it fair or healthy for our marriage if one of us exempts himself or herself from planning and deciding the course of the marriage out of some childish rejection of responsibility? Which of us does this?

7. *Entrapment.* This is especially annoying. A mate renigs on planning in order to "catch" the other in a mistake: "Well, it was your decision. I trusted you." I am amazed how some people continue to let their mates do this to them, even when they know the game. Occasionally it is a passive-aggressive way for one to "get" the other for a totally unconnected grievance. Questions: Do we ensnare or ambush each other with "Bang! I-got'cha" sick delight in the other's well-intentioned failure? And is one of us now gun-shy?

8. *Fear of failure.* This, of course, is probably the most universal reason for not planning. To think ahead, set goals, make plans, and take action only to have a failure is no fun. We resign ourselves to something called "fate," or "God's will," or "the best-laid plans of mice and men," or "something always happens anyway," and decide to drift in the name of absurdity, piety, spontaneity, or a raw, chin-into-the-wind courage that is sheer foolishness. Questions: Do we avoid planning by making poor excuses because we are terrified of failure? Do we cop out with a shoulder-shrugging acceptance of some sense of "what the hell" that rapes us of our power?

Preparing to Plan

1. *Recalling and sharing the past: What happened?*

We must embrace our past. We enrich each other with our own personal history, apart and together. Old memories surface again. Things buried are held up to the light for understanding. We inform the marriage with our adult "show-and-tell." We tell what hurt us and what felt good. Feelings are deepened, others released. We hear and touch each other's past and are thus better able to understand the present and plan the future.

Betty and John had been married two years after a short acquaintance and engagement. They were now talking seriously about having a baby. John saw that Betty could not really get her feelings into the conversations. When confronted she said, "You will be a great dad, but something is not ready yet. I would like to know *us* better. Not that I expect to find something that will change my mind about having a baby. I want that, but not yet. For example, I have never even met your grandparents, your mother's folks. Perhaps we should just fly out there and spend a few days with them. I have never talked for more than five minutes alone with your father. Your mother is like a stranger, except I think she likes me, and I know she enjoys really nice clothes. Oh, it's not that bad. But you don't know my folks either, not really. My parents knew each other's families for three generations. Don't you have the feeling that you would like to know more about where I'm coming from? I don't mean before we *dare* have a baby. In some ways knowing you better has absolutely *nothing* to do with having a baby, and in other ways it has *everything* to do with it. Do you know what I mean?"

Happily, John did. Some might say they should have done all this before marriage. Perhaps so. They had not. So now they took some time doing what John called a "little investigative reporting." They visited and talked, sharing impressions and feelings:

Okay, tell me about little boys. You were one once. What's the real low-down on those little guys? I've heard some strange things. *(Smiling)* If we ever have a boy, I want to be prepared.

Will you please tell me why the subject was always changed when your Uncle Jeff was mentioned?

My folks had a terrible fight one night. I cried myself to sleep. Next morning it was like nothing had happened. I was afraid to ask questions. I started worrying about us. I often had stomachaches. I'll never forget that night. Even now I don't like fights. They tear me up inside. I'll do anything not to rock the boat, and, as you say, that's not fair. I wilt on you sometimes.

Remember the night after our first date when you called me real late and my father was furious? Well, how would you like for me to tell you why he was so angry?

Since we got into this, I feel I have a whole library of short stories about us that begin "Let me tell you about the time." Sharing me and learning about you has been one of the most exciting things I've ever done.

2. *Checking out the present: What's happening?*

The past and future meet in the present. Since nothing new is happening in the past, and the future is yet "on the way," we live *now,* in the moment. We hold on to our history and welcome our arriving life today, in the present.

Therefore, couples need to stay current with one another and regularly ask of themselves, "What's happening to you, in you, around you, for you, and because of you? What is special about the life you are living, and how do you see me sharing it with you?"

We live as fish in a rich and teeming sea, and we are so much a part of the water that we cannot distinguish where sea ends and fish begin. Hence, we must be curious to sort out the tangled "now" of feelings and experiences by listening, reflecting, and interpreting together.

I've been watching you, and you're not reading that book at all. Is something bothering you?

What a party! Being your husband is a lot of fun!

I thought I had gotten over the blowup at work yesterday, but driving in this morning, I had an overwhelming urge to just keep on going. I felt I never wanted to see that office and those people again. Do you mind just talking about it with me? I've got to flush some stuff.

Please don't touch me that way. Here, put your hand under mine and follow me. There. See? That's better. Now, that's very nice. Very nice, indeed. Thank you. Now relax your mouth.

Waiting for you here took me back to when we were first dating. It seems so long ago. Just nine years. Does it seem long to you?

I know Jim's death was a terrible loss. Don't forget, I loved him too. But you just must not sit here and stare out the window, like you do so much. It has been almost two months since the funeral. Please talk to me.

Before we try to invent the future, we should attempt to get a clear fix on *now*. Recently, while leading a "Friends, Partners, and Lovers" workshop, I asked the couples to fantasize responses to this question: "If marriage is a house, what room are you in, and what's happening?" Following are a few of their answers. BEFORE YOU READ THEM, DO YOUR OWN FANTASY: Close your eyes and picture yourself in or about the house. What is happening that might reflect where you are and what's happening in your marriage?

Front Door

I can't seem to get in. The door is locked. It's cold and raining. There are no lights on inside. I feel lonely and depressed.

Living Room

Our family is sitting in front of the fireplace popping popcorn and telling favorite stories. Everyong is happy and teasing.

I am a life-size poster hanging on the wall over the fireplace. All the furniture is gone. No one is there. I slowly peel off the wall like a window shade and fall to the floor. I couldn't watch any more.

I am old, sitting in a rocking chair by a window. My cat is in the sun on the sill. Outside children are playing in the street. A little girl is watching them. She looks like me at eight. I feel sad. You see, I am only thirty-two, but I feel very old and quite young at the same time. Where is the now me, the real me? Worst of all, both of my people are just watching, not doing much of anything themselves. Both of me are only observing life. That's actually true, you know. John complains that I never want to do anything.

Dining Room

Our meals are a kind of communion. We talk and sing even at the table. The kids are small. We play guessing games after the meal. Nick does the dishes (Boy, that's a fantasy!) while the kids and I sit in a circle on the floor in the kitchen eating bowls of ice cream. (That seems silly.) Nick fusses. He has to walk around us and do the dishes while we just eat ice cream and laugh. Wow, I like that!

Bedroom

I am in bed with my wife. Sex is a big deal at our house. The kids are banging at the door. My wife and I are laughing so hard we can't do anything, or at least I can't.

My husband and I are in bed. This is where we most experience intimacy. He suddenly becomes a small boy, a baby, and then I am nursing him. Then he is himself again and we move to climax. The little boy, baby, parts bother me. He acts that way quite often. Even talks baby talk. I wish we could discuss that, but I am afraid I will hurt his feelings.

Bedtime with the children means stories, time to talk, songs, and prayers. We are all together—Tom, Eric, Rachael, and me—on Eric's bed this time. We are happy. I feel good. Simple as that.

I am asleep. That's all. In the fantasy I just watch me sleep. Since my husband's affair eight months ago, I am apt to sleep a lot, even though all that is over, and we have talked it all out. Should I be sleeping that much? Sometimes it scares me.

I am naked in front of my mirror. I am fat, maybe two hundred pounds. I actually weigh one thirty-six, although I "think fat" no matter what I weigh. My husband complains a lot. He says he knows when I gain even a couple of pounds. He's balding. Think I will tell him that.

Bathroom

I am sitting on the side of the tub, slumped over. The children are banging on the door. I am just sitting there crying. This is strange. I'd never do a thing like that to my children.

I am sitting in the tub with the shower going and the tub filling. I am at peace. I really dig hot water. I like to soak. My wife thinks all my bathing is not very masculine. She says I should go soak my head.

I am flushing the john over and over, but I can't seem to get everything to go down. It is like my marriage. Down the tube a little at a time, day after day. Six years flushed. I can't seem to take my hand off the handle.

Hall Closet

I hide in there like a little kid. I don't know what from. It's dark and I am scared. I hear my heart beating. A light starts going on and off. I see myself and then I can't. It's like strobing. I look different each time the light flashes. I get older. I open my eyes before I become a wrinkled old woman. I did not like this exercise. I do not recommend it for future workshops.

I am standing in the closet with the door closed, wearing my London Fog. Sherlock Holmes. I am spying on my wife. She comes in the house with my older brother. He opens the closet door and I strangle him. It is ghastly. I thought of opening my eyes, but had to see the end (ha!). My wife screamed and ran. Police came. I was arrested. My wife cried. When I got into the squad car, I looked back and saw her splitting her sides laughing. There is no truth in all this. I do not even have a brother. Could the "brother" be my mother's second husband? My real dad died. This guy looks real young for his age (48), and he gives my wife a lot of attention. This is stupid. Why did we do this fantasy thing?

Kitchen

I was cooking a fantastic meal. I like that room. I forget my problems there. I feel creative. Sometimes I even get the proverbial pat on the bottom by my wife. She did in the fantasy. I kissed her and left two big hand prints of flour on the back of her blue skirt, and she went out to work without knowing it. Fun fantasy. Like doing it. Think I'll try the hand part for real next time I cook bread and she's wearing a blue skirt. I think we have a real good marriage.

I am frying at the stove. It flames up. I run out the back door into my neighbor's arms. (He is here so do not read this aloud if you plan to.) He whirls me around and laughs. I am screaming fire, fire. But he keeps laughing and whirling me around. Firemen arrive and squirt water all over both of us and we fall apart. I remember my brother throwing water over two copulating dogs in our yard when I was little. This is an awful fantasy, but I can really see what you are getting at. This is too personal, but I wanted to share it with you. What do you think might happen if I told my husband this fantasy? I think I would feel better if I did. But I won't. At least not now.

Roof

I am on the roof like Santa—costume, deer, the works. I look at my watch. It is seconds before midnight, like the Cinderella story, too. I reach in my bag. It is empty except for this one doll. I drop it down the chimney and sail away in my sleigh. (This is really strange.) I am here with my wife. Sue does not know it, but I have decided to file for divorce. My wife is pregnant. I don't know what it all means. This fantasy has something to do with my decision, doesn't it?

Basement

Our "rec" room is transformed into a lovely ballroom with candles and everything, including a band. People are beautiful and dancing. I start down the stairs without any clothes on. My husband is at the bottom reaching out to me and smiling just as though I were dressed. I get halfway down and run crying back up the stairs. Everyone keeps dancing. My husband looks angry but does not follow me. I fall in a heap at the top sobbing. Then I see my husband dancing with a woman. It is me. I'm in both places. I don't understand, but I feel it is "right" for some reason. There is a truth about the fantasy. Me naked? Hmmmm! You said we could interpret them. I fear my husband knowing me really well. I don't want the lights on when we make love even. But I love him and we enjoy each other. Am I getting close? I am glad I did this particular fantasy. It is clearer now. We should talk about my fears. I know very well what I am afraid of. It's a thing that happened. That's my story. You've had your fantasy.

A fantasy often mirrors the unconscious for us and can reveal impressions, ideas, and feelings about our lives. Without allowing ourselves to become bewitched or obsessed with the pictures of our fantasy, we may still be instructed. Those who use the "marriage as a house" fantasy frequently find that the fantasy provokes an important inquiry into the thinking, feeling, acting, and believing patterns of their marriage.

In the above fantasies, it became clear to each person that the unconscious was offering a little piece of drama which depicted feelings, attitudes, and conditions in their lives and marriages. Some of these were obvious and clear. Others were more obscure and symbolic. The man who saw his life-size poster peel off the wall was having an affair. He felt phony and not really a part of his family, even though he feigned loyalty and dabbled in family activities. The fantasy simply drove home his lack of integrity and commitment. He later entered therapy alone, then with his wife. The affair was dissolved, and the imperiled marriage received a new lease on life. All of this might have happened without the fantasy. Yet, he referred to the fantasy as "the flash of lighting" that woke him up to what he was doing.

Other fantasies were more like looking at the family album of happy scenes. This can be reassuring, unless one decides that the fantasy is high comedy, a farce, as evidenced by some tone or note of unreality. After a fantasy of a beautiful family experience, one man exclaimed, "But it is never really that way. Is the fantasy a longing I have or does it point to our pretention? Our family has to look good." He was a minister. Still other fantasies—there are many of these—are explicitly sexual. These are frequently insightful, raising to awareness the buried loneliness or longing. Some simply reflect the joy of intimacy in the life of the couple.

Fantasies are messengers. Sometimes it takes courage to "answer the door" when a messenger knocks. But, almost without exception, the knock is worthy of your answering it, and the message is enlightening. "What's happening" may best be revealed in fantasy when you stop to get in touch with your unconscious on stage. Couples who learn to share their fantasies are more apt to make connections where others fail and at greater depths. Fantasy is at least one additional way to picture the present.

3. *Inventing the future: What's possible?*

Two fundamental questions that lead us into adult life, and keep measuring our progress, are the identity and destiny questions: Who am I? and Where am I going? We are already under way in this chapter with the destiny question as it applies to marriage: Where are *we* going? Do we go out to meet the future or wait for it to arrive? If we go out, what is our disposition? Are we anxious about the treachery of fate? Are we hostile and brewing for vengeance? Or are we excited about the challenge and the possibility of reward? Do we reach out to tomorrow and expect to call it "good"?

Hey, Sally, I overheard Hal on the phone today talking with a lawyer about drawing up a will. He's only thirty-six. Why would he need a will? That's creepy. *(Pause)* Do you ever think about getting old? About dying?

Jim and Sarah have moved into their new house. It's beautiful. Suppose we will ever live like that?

The strangest thing just happened. You know Jeff's little new friend, Michael? Well, he just asked me why we go to church every Sunday. I told him it was because we enjoy it. But that doesn't sound right. Now I'm wondering why we do go. When I was a kid, I was afraid I would die and go to hell if I didn't. We need to talk about church some time. I have a feeling it is more tied up with this trip we are on than I realized.

The law degree? That was years ago. I've given up on that. You have any idea how long that takes, and how much money? Besides, I'm ten years older than the kids in law school today. You're a crazy man, but I love you. *(Pause)* Mom would love taking care of Phillip for me, wouldn't she? And you did get that neat raise last month. No, it's ridiculous.

I think I would add ten years to my life if we just lived on a piece of lake-front property.

As a team we invent our future. We dream the possibilities of our destiny together. We are not the masters of our fate, but we might be the architects drawing the blueprints and the artists lifting life off the paper and giving it soul. That is quite a lot toward creating our lives.

Exercises

Try one or more of the following:

1. Write letters to each other, with three paragraphs beginning as follows:
    a. "If you and I continue as we are, in five years I can see us . . ."
    b. "However, if we have enough love and courage, we will . . ."

    c. "All of which can lead us into the life that I dream of for us, namely . . ."

Swap letters; read them carefully and discuss each paragraph. Note similarities and differences in the way you are seeing the future. Now what will you do about these fantasies? Find the action.

2. Divide a piece of writing paper into four equal parts. In each section write one of the four following headings:

    One-Year Goals

    Two-Year Goals

    Five-Year Goals

    Long-Range Goals

In each section list what you want to see accomplished by and for the two of you in each time frame. Be imaginative and willing to risk. Now exchange papers and compare dreams.

3. Answer the following questions:

    a. What is your best talent/skill?

    b. Does that talent/skill need and deserve improvement?

    c. How might you better express that talent/skill?

    d. Is there a market for it that could bring greater satisfaction and/or money?

    e. Would you really like to make your talent/skill a more central part of your life? Is so, how might you do this?

    f. Do you need a workable plan for organizing your life more effectively to deal with your talent/skill?

    g. If so, will you make a plan *now?* If not now, why not? When will you?

    h. How will you feel if you do nothing more than you are presently doing with your talent/skill?

    j. Is this talent/skill something that does or could enhance your marriage? If so, how?

    k. How does your mate feel about your talent/skill? How do other relatives and friends feel about it? (Support, tease, criticize, etc.?)

    l. If your plan works, what are the rewards? Sacrifices?

    m. So, if it works, will it all be worth the effort?

n. How might success affect your marriage?

o. If that first option does not work, where do you go from there to avoid getting caught in the win/lose syndrome we discussed earlier?

p. Stop right here. What are you now feeling? Is it a GO, STOP, or CAUTION feeling?

Now exchange papers and discuss FEELINGS carefully along with the answers and ideas. Ask: What does my mate seem most to need from me right now?

4. Think of your body moving through time and space. What sort of traveler are you? What sort is your mate? How able are these two to travel together? Following are some suggestions, but don't let these limit you. Find your own.

jaunter	runner
jogger	walker
charger	stroller
tiptoer	slider
crawler	cartwheeler
racer	tumbler
hopscotcher	swinger (Tarzan/Jane)
creeper	crawler
stumbler	floater
strider	

Is there something in the way you move together that will have a decisive impact on the way you do the future? Think about your rhythms, frequencies, postures, cadences. Are you more often in or out of "sync" with one another? How does this affect the action field of your marriage, especially as you look toward the future?

5. Do an art fantasy. You need four pieces of paper at least 8½" x 11," plus finger paints or colored pens, something with which to put color on a page. Let your fantasy soar. Do four pictures in this order with the following themes:

Where am I now?

What is the force or power that prevents me from changing?

What would enable or facilitate my changing?
What will I look like when I arrive?

After you have completed the series, get your mate's remarks before you try to "explain" your work. See what she or he "sees" first. Are you saying something "new" about yourself? Are the forms flowing or tight and meticulous? How do the colors make you feel? Is there significant "movement" in the process from the first to the fourth piece?

6. Play CHECKUP. Do this acrostic game with FUTURE.

F = Facts.	State facts about *now* with you. What are the positives and negatives?
U = Upset	Are you upset with the way things are? Check feelings: depression, anxiety, anticipation, urge to move on, anger, disappointment, etc. Just how "upset" are you, really?
T = Truth	Find the truth of what's possible. Now be honest with yourself. Shouldn't you play it safe and stay put? Who knows what's out there? What did you ever make happen by the sheer will of you? What is the truth of you as someone who makes things happen?
U = Ultimates	What are you after, finally? Complete the sentences: —"Sooner or later I want . . ." —"If I die without, . . ." —"Unless I get moving, . . ."
R = Resources	Name and measure on a scale of 1–10 your best resources, all of them that come to mind. What will it take to get to them and have them all working for you?
E = Enjoy	What pleasures can you anticipate from your dream? What permanent gain from the top options? What new discovery about you? What joy?

Swap your notes and see how the game informs you about the marriage. What do you have to share with one another? How do your dreams match? Where might you compromise? Can both achieve?

7. Fantasize together future trouble spots:

  a. A child "goofs up" or has a special need.

  b. Death or incapacity of a parent.

  c. Your retirement.

  d. Financial stress.

  e. Let your mind "float" through your family world and see where trouble spots and challenges stop you. Pay attention to these, no matter how farfetched your fantasy may seem. Discuss.

There is a great story coming out of the construction of the Frank Lloyd Wright house in Fallingwater, Pennsylvania. Word has it that when the day came to take down the beams that supported the enormous, cantilevered patios of great slabs of steel-reinforced concrete, the workmen refused because of the danger. Both the foreman and contractor failed to move the men to do the job. Finally, the architect himself arrived to persuade the workers. With a speech and blueprints he spoke of his knowledge of physics, stress factors, and the materials used. Their response said something like, "Yeah. Sure. But that down there is paper, and that up there is concrete." Finally, in exasperation, Wright grabbed a sledgehammer and began stalking up and down the rows of posts, smashing the supports, and breaking open the future with his bare hands as the workmen fled. Over him hung tons of concrete, as he bet his life on his dream. Today the building stands as a monument to the man and an important milepost in an evolving American architecture.

In a life worth living we are often betting our lives on our dreams. In marriage one mate may often seem like Frank Lloyd Wright risking great danger, perhaps destruction, while the other one trembles a bit at the audacity. Will it work? Are we crazy? Can we survive? In marriage it is best if both are building the dream, and both are tearing out the supports, partners in it all. Friends fantasize the future with an inventive humor. Lovers embrace their dream with a sense of mystery *and* fulfillment. Partners roll up their sleeves and get to work. It takes all three—friend, partner, lover—to make this union bring forth, again and again. Stretch, reach, and claim what is yours together.

BIBLIOGRAPHY

Allen, Gina, and Martin, Clement G., *Intimacy*. New York: Pocket Books, 1972.

Arieti, Silvano, *Creativity, the Magic Synthesis*. New York: Basic Books, Inc., Publishers, 1976.

Berne, Eric, *What Do You Say After You Say Hello?* New York: Grove Press, Inc., 1972.

Buber, Martin, *I and Thou*, trans. Walter Kaufman. New York: Charles Scribner's Sons, 1970.

Comfort, Alex, *The Joy of Sex*. New York: Crown Publishers, Inc., 1972.

_____, *More Joy of Sex*. New York: Crown Publishers, Inc., 1975.

Frankl, Viktor, E. *Man's Search for Meaning*, rev. ed. Boston: Beacon Press, 1963.

Fromm, Erich, *The Art of Loving*. New York: Harper & Row, Publishers, Inc., 1956.

153

Hamachek, Don E., *Encounters with Self*. New York: Ho
and Winston, 1971.

Hillman, James, *Insearch: Psychology and Religion*.
Charles Scribner's Sons, 1967.

Hite, Shere, *The Hite Report*. New York: Dell Publishin
1977.

Johnson, Robert A., *She!* King of Prussia, Pa.: Religious
Company, 1976.

————, *He!* King of Prussia, Pa.: Religious Publishing
1974.

Lowen, Alexander, *Pleasure*. New York: Penguin Book

Mace, David and Vera, *We Can Have Better Marriages I
Want Them*. Nashville: Abingdon Press, 1974.

————, *How to Have a Happy Marriage*. Nashville
Press, 1977.

Maslow, Abraham H., *Religions, Values and Peak E*
Columbus, Ohio: Ohio State University Press, 1964.

Masters, William H., et al, *The Pleasure Bond: A Ne*
Sexuality and Commitment. Boston: Little, Brown &
1975.

May, Rollo, *Love and Will*. New York: W. W. Norton &
1969.

————, *The Courage to Create*. New York: W. W. Nor
Inc., 1975.

Molton, Warren Lane, *Bruised Reeds*. Valley Forge: Jud
1970.

Neale, Robert E., *In Praise of Play*. New York: Harp
Publishers, Inc., 1969.

Riesman, David, *The Lonely Crowd*. New Haven: Yale
Press, 1961.

Rogers, Carl, *On Becoming a Person*. Boston: Houghton Mifflin Company, 1961.

_____, *Becoming Partners: Marriage and Its Alternatives*. New York: Delacorte Press, 1972.

Singer, Jerome L., *The Inner World of Daydreaming*. New York: Harper & Row, Publishers, Inc., 1975.

Steiner, Claude, *Scripts People Live*. New York: Grove Press, Inc., 1974.

Stevens, John O., *Awareness: Exploring, Experimenting, Experiencing*. Lafayette, Calif.: Real People Press, 1971.

INDEX